Marx: A Clear Guide

Marx: A Clear Guide

Edward Reiss

Pluto Press

LONDON · CHICAGO, ILLINOIS

First published 1997 by Pluto Press
345 Archway Road, London N6 5AA
and 1436 West Randolph, Chicago, Illinois 60607, USA

Copyright © Edward Reiss 1997

British Library Cataloguing in Publication Data
A catalogue record for this book is available from the British Library

ISBN 0 7453 1015 X hbk

Library of Congress Cataloging in Publication Data
Reiss, Edward.
    Marx : a clear guide / Edward Reiss.
        p.   cm.
    Includes bibliographical references and index.
    ISBN 0–7453–1015–X (hbk.)
    1. Marx, Karl, 1818–1883. 2. Communists—Biography.
3. Socialism—History. 4. Communism—History. I. Title.
HX39.5.R35   1996
335.4—dc20   96–28836
                                                                          CIP

Reprinted with corrections 1998

Designed and produced for Pluto Press by
Chase Production Services, Chipping Norton, OX7 5QR
Typeset from disk by Stanford DTP Services, Milton Keynes
Printed in the EC by Redwood Books, Trowbridge

With thanks to
my family and friends

Contents

Introduction

Overview

This is a very clear introduction to Marx. It calls a spade a spade, not a determinate implement in the pre-bourgeois agricultural production process.

The book starts with Marx as a human being – private life and public life. It then presents his main ideas in a way that is as simple as possible, but not any simpler. It bypasses the secondary literature; returns to Marx's original work; explains and criticises it; and says which parts are dead and which are still relevant.

At the end are three appendices. The first – 'The Attraction of Marxism' – is written for those who wonder 'what's so good about Marx anyway?' The second, called 'Violence, Negativity and Failure', deals with the important question: 'Did Marx lead on to Stalin?' The third gives detailed references for further reading.

Why Study Marx?

Marx is, to use one of his own terms, a 'world-historical' individual. This means that his life is linked up with world history. To understand Marx is to understand a good deal about the nineteenth century: capitalism, colonialism, social and ideological change, etc.

Marx plays an equally important role in the twentieth century. He is the spectre at the heart of its major movements: the rise and fall of socialism, the Cold War and anti-colonial revolution in the Third World. He is the man behind Lenin, Stalin, Trotsky, Gramsci, Mao Tse Tung and Fidel Castro.

Much of the intellectual history of this century also revolves around Marx. Think of European philosophy: Sartre, Camus, existentialism, the Frankfurt School, modernism, postmodernism and poststructuralism. Marx influenced artists (Picasso, Matisse), poets (Louis Aragon, Paul Eluard, André Breton, Pablo Neruda), writers (Maxim Gorky, Sean O'Casey, George Orwell), dramatists (Bertold Brecht, Arthur Miller), film-makers (Buñuel, Eisenstein, Charlie Chaplin) and all-rounders (William Morris, G.B. Shaw, Paul Robeson).

It takes a great thinker to make a great mistake. Marx tackled the big issues (poverty and injustice) and he asked the big questions: what is the purpose of study? what is the relationship between thought and action? why are we as we are? how do we change the world? etc. Even if he got wrong answers, at least his thought was ambitious, creative and critical. Criticising him in turn helps to stretch, sharpen and clarify one's own thinking. The challenge is to separate the positive, constructive, live part of Marx's work from the negative and the dead.

Marx is an interdisciplinary thinker *par excellence*. His main subject was capitalism, its strengths and weaknesses, and, now capitalism seems all-triumphant, that subject is more important than ever. More generally, he studied

- power;
- why some are rich and some poor;
- the dynamics, or 'laws of motion', of history;
- the interaction between science, economics and life;
- how technology creates social change;
- how societies reproduce themselves;
- how societies change;
- globalisation and the significance of new technologies;
- ideology: or the relationship between ideas and society.

Rightly or wrongly, Marx's thought is a major reference point in history, philosophy, literature, sociology and economics, as well as in studies of culture, media and international relations. If you know *exactly* where you stand in relation to Marx – where you agree and disagree with him – you will be well placed in all these fields.

Marx is an exhilarating thinker, a man of great insights and colossal mistakes. After 1917, the polarisation of opinion was such that, practically speaking, you were either for him or against him; little else was possible. With the end of the Cold War, new interpretations come to light. This Guide neither demonises nor idolises Marx. It discusses both his achievements and his errors; and tries to convey the colourfulness, diversity and exuberance of his writing, its passion and vitality.

CHAPTER 1

A Private Life

Academics in general and Marxist ones in particular have tended to overlook Marx's private life, as if it were inconsequential. Is it?

Synopsis

1818	Marx is born – in Trier, an ancient market town in the Rhineland, Germany.
	His family is relatively well-off. His father is a lawyer who has given up the Jewish faith in order to gain recognition. He gives Karl a taste for Racine and the works of the French Enlightenment, Rousseau and Voltaire.
	Learns aspects of Jewish culture, especially from his mother.
	Acquires a love for the German Romantics, also of Homer, Dante and Shakespeare, from a neighbour, the Baron von Westphalen. The Baron is a liberal, who sympathises with the ideals of the French utopian socialist, Saint-Simon.
	The Baron's daughter, Jenny, 'the most beautiful girl in Trier', four years older than Marx, becomes engaged to him.
	As a student Karl writes love lyrics to Jenny, drinks, duels, runs up large debts and works himself to exhaustion.
1843	Karl and Jenny marry. They move to Paris, there to mix in radical, cosmopolitan circles, along with the poets Herwegh and Heine and the Russian anarchist, Bakunin.
1844–57	Jenny has seven children. Four die young.
1845	Marx expelled from France. Renounces his Prussian nationality. Announces himself a 'citizen of the world'.
1848	Marx inherits 6,000 francs and (according to the police at least) gives 5,000 to buy weapons for the workers in Brussels. Belgian police unhappy. Marx expelled from Belgium.
1849	Marx on trial in Cologne for inciting armed rebellion. Acquitted. Expelled from Germany ... and Paris.

Karl and Jenny come to live in London, often in poverty, with their young children and their friend and housekeeper, Hélène Demuth.

London then is a huge city, with 2.5 million people, perhaps the most prosperous city in the world, though with great poverty. It is the London of Dickens, the London which Cobbett called 'the great wen'.

In sadly straitened circumstances, Jenny tries to cash in on her aristocratic pedigree, printing her visiting card: 'Mrs Karl Marx, née Baroness Jenny von Westphalen'. Her family were distant relatives of the Dukes of Argyll, whose crest was emblazoned on her silverware.

Times were hard. Marx made frequent visits to the pawn shop. Has to explain how he got the silver.

Marx family evicted by bailiffs in front of a watching crowd.

1850–56   Move to two cramped rented rooms in Soho, London. Marx was constantly in debt. Engels would send £5 notes, cut in two and posted in separate letters.[1] (They suspected their post was intercepted.)

1850   Marx secures a ticket for the British Museum Library. Starts off by reading back numbers of *The Economist*.

'In the early summer 1851', Jenny wrote, 'an event occurred which I do not wish to relate here in detail, although it greatly contributed to increase our worries, both personal and others.'[2]

Her husband had fathered an illegitimate child with Hélène Demuth (known in the family as 'Lenchen'). The scandal is hushed up and the child, Freddy Demuth, fostered out.

Other children of Marx and Jenny die in infancy (malnutrition and poverty).

Three daughters survive: Jenny, Laura and Eleanor.

1856   Jenny inherits some money. The family rents a better, terrace house, with its own bathroom and toilet, in a lower-middle-class area, on the edge of Kentish Town, or, as Jenny puts it, 'not far from lovely Hampstead Heath'.[3]

The children go to school at the South Hampstead College for Ladies. Money is soon spent. The furniture returns to the pawn shop.[4]

Marx is adamant. 'I have got to pursue my object through thick and thin and not allow bourgeois society to turn me into a MONEY-MAKING MACHINE.'[5]

He takes refuge in algebra, maths and Thucydides.[6]

He works late into the night, dosed on lemonade and tobacco.[7]

His health suffers. Afflicted with all kinds of illness, including boils and furuncles.

1860   Jenny contracts smallpox. Survives, scarred and blotchy, looking like 'a rhinoceros, a hippopotamus'.[8]

1861   Marx loses his chief source of income, articles for the *New York Daily Tribune*, which no longer wanted him as a European correspondent, due to the American Civil War. Tries for a job at a railway office. 'Luckily – or perhaps I should say unluckily? – I did not get the post because of my bad handwriting.'[9]

It was Jenny who copied out his long, scrawled papers into legible scripts for the publishers.

1864   Two legacies. They move to a larger, detached house. Throw a ball.

Money troubles recommence.

1870   Engels retires and gives Marx a pension of £350 a year.

1871   Marx, whose fame has hitherto been restricted to a small circle of revolutionaries, writes in defence of the Paris Commune. Suddenly he gains public notoriety as 'the notorious Karl Marx' and 'the Red Terror Doctor'.[10]

1874   Applies for British citizenship. Application rejected by authorities.

1881   Jenny dies from cancer of the liver.

1883   Marx's eldest daughter dies. He follows two months later. Lenchen goes to work for Engels.

1890   Lenchen dies. Buried in the same grave as Karl and Jenny, in Highgate Cemetery, near the novelist George Eliot and Herbert Spencer, who wrote 'socialism is slavery'.

Sample Correspondence

London, 8 September 1852
28 Dean Street, Soho

Dear Engels,

Your letter today found us in a state of great agitation.

My wife is ill. Little Jenny is ill. Lenchen has some sort of nervous fever. I could not and cannot call the doctor because I have no money to buy medicine. For the past 8–10 days I have been feeding the FAMILY solely on bread and potatoes, but whether I shall be able to get hold of any today is doubtful ... .

The best and most desirable thing that could happen would be for the LANDLADY to throw me out. Then I would at least be quit of the sum of £22. But such complaisance is hardly to be expected of her. On top of that debts are still outstanding to the baker, the milkman, the tea chap, the GREENGROCER, the butcher. How am I to get out of this infernal mess ... .

You'll have seen from my letters that, as usual, when I myself am in the shit and not just hearing about it at second-hand, I plough through it with complete indifference ... .

Your K.M.[11]

(The next day, Marx received £4 from Engels)

Sayings

'I am not a Marxist.'[12]

'Work for humanity.'[13]

'I am a citizen of the world. I am active wherever I am.'[14]

'*Capital* will not even pay for the cigars I smoked writing it.'[15]

'Children should educate their parents.'[16]

'I am a machine condemned to devour [books] and then throw them, in a changed form, on the dunghill of history.'[17]

'Go on your way and let tongues wag.'[18]

'There is only one effective antidote for mental suffering and that is physical pain. Set the end of the world on the one hand against a man with acute toothache on the other.'[19]

Snapshots

Once a gentleman asked [Marx] who would clean shoes in the future state. He answered vexedly, 'You should.'[20]

[Marx, aged 28] was of medium height, broad-shouldered, powerful in build and energetic in his deportment. His brow was high and finely shaped, his hair thick and pitch-black, his gaze piercing. His mouth already had the sarcastic line that his opponents feared so much ... .[21]

Marx was an excellent draughts player. He was so expert at the game that it was difficult to beat him at all. He enjoyed chess too, but he was not so skilful at it. He tried to make up for that by zeal and surprise attacks.[22]

Spy in Soho

Jenny's brother, who happened to be the Prussian Minister of the Interior, despatched a crack agent, the future head of Bismarck's secret service, to investigate the Marx family, who, at the time, were holed up in two rented rooms in Soho. The agent reported back that Marx often 'lounges about doing nothing for days on end, but if there is anything which must be done he works day and night with tireless energy. He has no notion of keeping regular hours.' The apartment was 'broken, shabby and ragged and there is the greatest muddle everywhere'.

In the middle of the living room there is a big table covered with oilcloth. On it are piled his manuscripts, books and papers; the children's toys; his wife's sewing; chipped tea-cups; dirty spoons, knives and forks; lamps, an inkwell, glasses, claypipes, tobacco ash; in a word, it is the most indescribable muddle – and all on the one table. When one goes into the room one's eyes are so blinded by coal and tobacco smoke that it is like walking about in a cave until one becomes accustomed to it and objects begin to loom up through the fog ... . One of the chairs has only three legs; and the children are playing at cooking on another one which happens to be whole, and which they offer to the guest; so if you sit down it is at the risk of ruining your trousers.[23]

Snippets

At home, the Marx family were known by nick-names:

Table 1.1: Marx family nick-names

Karl Marx	Moor, Challey, Old Nick, Doctor Crankey
Jenny Marx	Möhmchen, Mummelchen, Memeliten
Hélène Demuth	Lenchen, Nym
Jenny Marx (daughter)	Quiqui, Emperor of China, Di, Jennychen, Schwärzchen (dark one)
Laura Marx	The Hottentot, Kakadou, The Secretary
Eleanor Marx	Tussy, Quoquo, Successor to the Emperor of China, Getwerg Alberich, Miss Lilliput
Engels	The General

Marx's name 'Moor' refers to his swarthy complexion and also recalls Shakespeare's Othello, the 'Moor of Venice', noted for his gullibility and chivalry ... .

Self-disclosures

Below are the 'confessions' of Marx and his daughter, which show something of their values and tastes.

Table 1.2: Self-disclosures of Karl and Jenny Marx

Confessions	Karl Marx (1865)[24]	Jenny Marx (1867)[25]
Favourite virtue	Simplicity	Humanity
Favourite virtue in man	Strength	Moral courage
Favourite virtue in woman	Weakness	Devotion
Your chief characteristic	Singleness of purpose	Not asked
Your idea of happiness	To fight	Not answered
Your idea of misery	Submission	Not answered
The vice you excuse most	Gullibility	Prodigality
The vice you detest most	Servility	Envy
Your aversion	Martin Tupper[a]	Knights, priests, soldiers
Favourite occupation	Book-worming	Reading
Characters of history I most dislike	Not asked	Bonaparte and his nephew
Favourite poet	Shakespeare, Aeschylus, Goethe	Shakespeare
Favourite prose-writer	Diderot	Cervantes
Favourite composer	Not asked	Handel, Beethoven, Wagner[b]
Favourite hero	Spartacus,[c] Kepler[d]	Not asked
Favourite heroine	Gretchen[e]	Not asked
Favourite flower	Daphne	Not asked
Favourite colour	Red	Red
Favourite name	Laura, Jenny	Not asked
Favourite dish	Fish	Not asked
Favourite maxim	Nihil humani a me alienum puto[f]	To thine own self be true
Favourite motto	De omnibus dubitandum[g]	Alle für Einen, Einer für Alle[h]

a Sententious, didactic versifier, author of *Proverbial Philosophy*.
b Jenny had just heard Wagner for the first time, in Hanover.
c Leader of Roman slave uprising.
d German astronomer.
e From Goethe's *Faust*.
f 'I think nothing human is alien from me.'
g 'Doubt everything.'
h 'All for one and one for all.'

Marx's other literary favourites included Homer, the *Arabian Nights*, Dante, Cervantes, Goethe, Heine, Balzac, Alexander Dumas senior, Walter Scott, Henry Fielding (especially *Tom Jones*) and Robbie Burns.

Studies

Marx wrote in German, French and English. He also knew ancient Greek, Latin, Spanish and Russian, with some Italian and Turkish. 'A foreign language', he would say, 'is a weapon in the struggle of life.'[26]

> He had the habit of going through his notebooks and reading the passages underlined in the books after intervals of many years in order to keep them fresh in his memory. He had an extraordinarily reliable memory which he had cultivated from his youth according to Hegel's advice by learning by heart verse in a foreign language he did not know.[27]

Marx kept up with new discoveries in physics and chemistry. He especially admired Darwin's *Origin of Species* (1859) and hoped to do for social and political science what Darwin had achieved in natural science.

Questions

1. What, if any, of the information above is significant for understanding Marx?
2. Do you find the portrait of Marx which emerges from these accounts attractive, alarming or what?

CHAPTER 2

A 'World-historical' Life

Many historians now think that the 'Industrial Revolution' was actually more an 'Industrial Evolution'. Whichever it was, it had taken off in Britain and was spreading in Europe, during Marx's life. Country people were being forced off the land and into cities and slums. The gap between rich and poor widened. Socialists argued that the workers did the work, but the owners ('capitalists') took the profit. Marx himself became a communist around 1844.

The chronology below shows some land-mark dates in Marx's life and in the development of his ideas. You can read it rather like a newspaper, either flicking through to get a general idea of what was going on, or more carefully to see the details.

1818	Born.
1835	Studies law in the university town of Bonn.
1836	Studies philosophy in Berlin, capital of Prussia and the city of the German philosophical giant, Hegel. Joins the 'Doctors' Club', which debates Hegelian philosophy.
Early 1840s	Influenced by Feuerbach with his humanist critique of Hegel. Argues that 'God' is an externalised alien, a figment of the imagination on to which we project our humanity.
1841	Becomes a Doctor of Philosophy, with a thesis on Ancient Greek philosophy.
1842–43	Edits a progressive newspaper in Cologne, the *Rheinische Zeitung*. 'The Free Press ... is the spiritual mirror in which a people can see itself, and self-examination is the first condition of wisdom' (*CW*, 1, 164–5).
1843	Marries and moves to Paris.
1844	In Paris, Marx meets French communists. Also Engels, who becomes his life-long friend and benefactor. Publishes a review journal, the *Deutsch-Französische Jahrbücher*. The first volume (which, as things turn out, is also the last) is banned in Prussia. It includes poems by Herwegh and Heine,

a major article by Engels ('Outlines of a Critique of Political Economy') and two pieces by Marx: *On the Jewish Question*, 'Money is the estranged essence of man's work and man's existence, and this alien essence dominates him, and he worships it' (*CW*, 3, 172).

'Contribution to the Critique of Hegel's *Philosophy of Right* [Recht]: Introduction' 'Religion ... is the *opium* of the people' (*CW*, 3, 175).

Marx also writes *Economic and Philosophic Manuscripts*. Criticises orthodox economics on the grounds that it (a) assumes capitalism is natural and eternal and thereby (b) connives in the exploitation of workers.

1844–45	Marx develops the 'materialist theory of history'. (Crudely put, changes in technology cause changes in society which cause changes in ideology. It tries to explain big social changes in the 'mode of production': how society evolves from hunter-gatherers, through Graeco-Roman slave states and feudalism, to capitalism.) Begins to brew his distinctive revolutionary cocktail: a potent brew of German philosophy, French socialism and British political economy.
1845	'Theses on Feuerbach': 'The philosophers have only interpreted the world in various ways; the point is to change it' (*CW*, 5, 5). Engels publishes *The Condition of the Working Class in England*, a graphic account of poverty in Manchester. Marx joins the League of the Just. He and Engels set up 'Communist Corresponding Committees' (1846), which merge into the 'Communist League' (1847).
1845–46	Marx and Engels co-write *The Holy Family* and *The German Ideology* (not published until 1932). These set out their own materialist theories and, at inordinate length, criticise 'Young Hegelian' philosophers.
1847	*The Poverty of Philosophy*. A polemic against the leading French socialist, Proudhon. Marx summarises his theory about the importance of technology in shaping society. 'The handmill gives you society with the feudal lord; the steam mill, society with the industrial capitalist' (*CW*, 6, 166).

A financial crash and rising prices prepare the way for 1848.

1848   A year of revolutions. Working-class insurrections across Europe.

Marx publishes *The Communist Manifesto*.

Edits a new newspaper in Cologne: the *Neue Rheinische Zeitung*. Organises mass meetings.

Uprisings suppressed.

1849   Marx on trial in Cologne, charged with incitement to rebellion. Acquitted.

Newspaper banned. Marx brings out a final edition in red letters.

Expelled from Germany, Belgium and France, Marx arrives as an exile in London. Works on relief committees to support other refugees.

Wage Labour and Capital (a basic introduction to his economic ideas).

1850   Marx sets up a radical monthly, the *Neue Rheinische Zeitung-Revue*. Analyses recent events in France. His articles are reprinted by Engels in 1895 as 'The Class Struggles in France.'

'Address to the Communist League': 'The arming of the whole proletariat with rifles, muskets, cannon, and ammunition must be carried out at once ...' (*CW*, 10, 283).

1851   Year of the Great Exhibition, at the Crystal Palace, a show-case of prosperity. Symbolises the confidence of the British ruling class in technology, trade and Empire.

In France, Louis Napoleon, a nephew of the famous Napoleon Bonaparte, stages a coup d'état and sets up as a dictator, Napoleon III. Hopes of a socialist revolution are quashed.

1852   Marx again analyses what has gone 'wrong' in France and vents his frustration in an electrifying pamphlet, *The Eighteenth Brumaire of Louis Bonaparte*.

Communist League dissolved.

October. Marx's comrades tried for high treason in Cologne. Most get off with sentences of several years.

1850s and 1860s   Marx works on his economics. 'The whole thing is divided into six books. 1. Capital. 2. Landed Property. 3. Wage Labour. 4. The State. 5. International Trade. 6. World Market' (Marx,

1858, *CW*, 40, 270). He never completed the latter topics.

In the thick of communist politics, Marx also writes articles for various papers, especially (1852–61) for the *New York Daily Tribune*. His articles give background analysis on current affairs.

1857   *Grundrisse*, draft notes for his economics (first published 1939–41).

Another financial crash disturbs the prosperity of mid-Victorian England, but, this time, does not spark off revolutionary uprisings.

1857–58   Writes articles for the *New American Cyclopedia*.

1859   *Contribution to the Critique of Political Economy*. The preface summarises his materialist conception of history – 'historical materialism'.

Darwin publishes his *Origin of Species*, about evolution and natural selection. Marx hopes that his own 'scientific' theories will emulate Darwin's.

1860   *Herr Vogt*, a long tirade against a critic.

1861   Emancipation of the Russian serfs.

1861–65   American Civil War. Marx supports the North, against the Southern slave-holders (even though the halt to cotton imports puts cotton workers in England out of work).

Meanwhile, Bismarck is setting about the unification of Germany.

1861–3   Marx is hard at work. Produces 23 hefty notebooks. Some of this reappears in *Capital*, Vol. I; some is edited by Engels, as *Capital*, Vol. III; some is extracted by Kautsky as *Theories of Surplus Value*.

1864   Starts the International Workingmen's Association, the 'First International'. 'Workers of the world, Unite!' Marx writes the Inaugural Address and Statutes and generally acts as *éminence grise*.

1865   'Value, Price and Profit'. Marx summarises his economic theories for the benefit of others in the First International.

1867   *Das Kapital*, vol. 1. Marx's *chef-d'oeuvre*.

The Reform Act extends the vote to many working men.

1870–71   Marx teaches himself Russian. His ideas are catching on there (and Russian is the first language into which *Kapital* is translated).

Franco–Prussian War. Shows strength of nationalist, not class, feelings.

1871

January   The Prussians take Paris after a four-month siege.

March   Citizens of Paris rise up and establish the Commune.

April   Their opponents, led by Thiers, at Versailles, start to bombard Paris.

May   Commune suppressed. 20,000 Communards killed.

August   Thiers elected President of France.

    Marx records this – and his hopes and visions – in *The Civil War In France*. He portrays the Commune as a prototype of socialist society.

1872   After splits with Bakunin and anarchists, Marx has the First International moved to New York, where it withers away and is formally terminated in 1876.

1874–75   Marx reads and criticises Bakunin's book, *Statism and Anarchy*, about the dangers of bureaucracy and a new elite in a post-revolutionary state. Marx dismisses his fears.

1875   *Critique of the Gotha Programme*. Marx criticises the programme of the German Social Democrat party and briefly outlines his own ideas of steps towards socialism.

1878   Engels' *Anti-Dühring* popularises Marx's ideas, which are now starting to spread, especially in Russia.

1880   'Questionnaire'. Marx seeks data from French workers on their working conditions.

1883   Marx dies.

    He leaves a mass and mess of unpublished manuscripts. Engels takes on their editing.

1884   Engels, *Origins of the Family, Private Property and the State*.

1885   *Capital*, Volume II, edited by Engels.

1889   The Second International is established.

1891   In Britain, Keir Hardie founds the Independent Labour Party.

1894   *Capital*, Volume III, edited by Engels.

1895   Engels dies. Plekhanov and Kautsky take over as leading spokesmen for 'Marxism'.

1905   First (failed) Russian revolution.

1905–10   Kautsky publishes Marx's *Theories of Surplus Value*, itself 3 volumes long, but also known as Volume IV of *Capital*.

1914   The First World War starts.
                      The Second International splits. Most delegates
                  support their own country, rather than ideals of
                  socialist internationalism.
1917   Lenin's Bolsheviks seize power.

CHAPTER 3

Unhappiness and Alienation

This chapter

- explains what is meant by alienation;
- shows the different ways Marx used the word;
- suggests some alternative explanations for unhappiness;
- demonstrates that the concept, mainly associated with his early 'humanist' period, is also important in his 'mature' work;
- asks whether it is still a useful concept today.

The Experience

Alienation can be understood as an *experience* of feeling dehumanised, when human needs go unmet. It may involve stress, exhaustion, poverty and chronic lack of fulfilment. What Marx had in mind by 'alienation' can be understood most starkly by imagining the reality facing a worker in a Victorian factory.

Nowadays the word 'alienation' might be used to describe the life of manual workers, students, home-makers or the under-class or shanty-dwellers in the 'Third World'. It could also be applied to the routine and resignation of commuters, mentally exhausted, emotionally numbed, spiritually deadened ... .

> Unreal city,
> Under the brown fog of a winter dawn,
> A crowd flowed over London Bridge, so many,
> I had not thought death had undone so many.
> Sighs, short and infrequent, were exhaled
> And each man fixed his eyes before his feet ... .[1]

The Concept

Alienation can also be seen as a *theory* of unhappiness. For if, as believed by the nineteenth-century thinkers known as Utilitarians, everyone seeks to maximise their own happiness, then we have to add that most people fail miserably.

Marx uses the term 'alienation' in several different ways, to refer to:

- the facts of inequality. A small group of people own factories, etc.; the large mass of workers do not. In general, the people who work in a factory do not own it: the person who owns it does not work there.
- the workers' subsequent obligation to sell to the capitalist their time, energy and skills (their 'labour power').[2] In the absence of unemployment benefit, they are compelled to choose between work or destitution. As Marx puts it, 'masses of men have nothing to sell but their labour power ... they are compelled to sell themselves voluntarily'.[3]
- In their work, the workers are therefore dependent and disempowered, forced to labour 'under the dominion, the coercion, and the yoke of another man'.[4]
- This, plus capitalist competition, creates bad, dehumanising conditions. Profits come before people. Competition increases productivity, but also pressure. The worker's activity 'belongs to another; it is the loss of his self'.[5]
- The worker's product is also taken away. It goes to the capitalist. 'Labour's product confronts it as *something alien, as a power independent* of the producer.'[6]
- This amounts to a 'Catch 22': the workers' labour only strengthens the system which oppresses them. Their work (a) makes the rich richer and more powerful and (b) makes society more consumerist and money-oriented. The harder workers labour, the greater grows the power that oppresses them. They become cogs in the system, bricks in the wall.
- Work lacks meaning and satisfaction. People are alienated from what they have done – the 'product of their labour'. They feel tied to soul-destroying, dead-end jobs. ('You work all day and what do you get? Another day older and deeper in debt.')
- People feel cut off or 'estranged' from each other. They see others as rivals for scarce resources.
- Workers are also restricted by the particular area of specialism required for their job. We become robots or trained gorillas. We do not develop our full human potential.
- Reacting to the above, people may feel:
  - dwarfed, powerless, isolated, trapped, thwarted;
  - confused, dissatisfied, victimised, used;
  - angry, abusive, aggressive;
  - exhausted, cynical, depressed, apathetic.

These are the subjective aspects of 'alienation'.

Clearly, several of Marx's usages overlap. He does not specify the exact meaning in each particular case. He uses the word 'alienation' to refer to a common experience and explain it in a particular way. The concept is both analytic and rhetorical (in the sense that it is intended to persuade us and alter our perceptions). 'Alienation' is a philosophical term, used to describe a socioeconomic and psychological condition, for political ends, with moral and rhetorical force. Below we can see several instances of how Marx uses the word.

> What, then, constitutes the alienation of labour?
> First, the fact that labour is *external* to the worker, i.e., it does not belong to his intrinsic nature; that in his work, therefore, he does not affirm himself but denies himself, does not feel content but unhappy, does not develop freely his physical and mental energy, but mortifies his body and ruins his mind.[7]

Marx asserts (above) that the labour done 'does not belong to [the worker's] intrinsic nature'. We might take this to mean that the workers are forced to work (by the external reality of poverty); would not do this work, given the choice; lack control over hours, work practices and conditions; and have no say in the product and how it will be used. Their days are sacrificed for something meaningless or even hostile.

For Marx this state is not inevitable. He implies that under different social conditions, the worker could 'affirm himself', 'feel content' and 'develop freely his physical and mental energy'. Work might become a positive 'human function'. In a truly human society, work would satisfy genuine human needs; create positive connections between people; and become an expression and proof of the individual's personality.[8] This is an optimistic, humanist vision. We long for self-realisation and self-fulfilment, but since most available jobs are tedious, degrading or dehumanising, people can only really be themselves outside the work-place. When the working day ends, life begins, 'at table, in the public house, in bed'.[9]

Various aspects of alienated experience, along with the anger and resistance of the immigrant manual labourer, are expressed in the song below.

> mi use to work dig ditch w'en it cowl no bitch
> mi did strang like a mule, but, bwoy, mi did fool
> den awftah a while mi jus' stap dhu ovahtime
> den awftah a while mi jus' phu dung mi tool
>
> well mi dhu day wok an' mi dhu nite wok
> mi dhu clean wok an' mi dhu dutty wok
> dem say dat black man is very lazy
> but if y'u si how mi wok y'u woulda say mi crazy

dem haffi a lickle facktri up inna Brackly
inna disya facktri all dem dhu is pack crackry
fi di laas fifteen years dem get me laybah
now awftah fifteen years mi fall out a fayvah

Inglan is a bitch ... .[10]

Marx's claims about 'alienation' prompt several questions:

- Were they true at the time of writing?
- Are they true today, when people (in the advanced industrial countries at least) have more leisure, more disposable income and better conditions at work?
- Is someone who is unemployed still alienated?
- Does Marx underestimate the extent to which people can be satisfied by their life outside work, family life, etc.?
- If dull jobs still have to be done under socialism, or even communism, does this invalidate Marx's theory?
- Do people really *need* to relate to what they produce?

Some of Marx's writing on alienation looks like dated and extravagant polemic from an era of early industrialism.

It is true that labour produces wonderful things for the rich – but for the worker it produces privation. It produces palaces – but for the worker hovels. It produces beauty – but for the worker deformity.[11]

Marx sees alienation as not just an extreme condition, but one which encompasses all conditions of work – clean and dirty, safe and dangerous – under capitalism. What the worker produces, Marx claims, becomes an 'alien power'.

The *alienation* of the worker in his product means not only that his labour becomes an object, an *external* existence, but that it exists *outside him,* independently, as something alien to him, and that it becomes a power on its own confronting him. It means that the life which he has conferred on the object confronts him as something hostile and alien.[12]

This assertion is easy to understand in some cases, like a worker in a police state who makes electronic stun truncheons or tear gas. It is less easy to understand how if someone makes toothpaste, this object later confronts them as 'something hostile and alien'. But it is Marx's contention that the products of labour are alienated in that they strengthen the position of the capitalists. It follows that increased wealth and commodity production may increase rather than reduce the world of alienation. Prosperity and consumer choice are not necessarily enough.

The worker becomes all the poorer the more wealth he produces, the more his production increases in power and size. The worker becomes an ever cheaper commodity the more commodities he creates. The *devaluation* of the world of men is in direct proportion to the *increasing value* of the world of things. Labour produces not only commodities: it produces itself and the worker as a *commodity* – and this at the same rate at which it produces commodities in general.[13]

Marx is objecting to the fundamental condition which forces the worker to work for a capitalist. According to Marx this leads to the devaluation of the human, by turning the worker into a commodity, someone who can be bought and sold as a worker.

Alienation is exacerbated by the 'division of labour'. This means that people are told to specialise: to develop some parts of our personality at the expense of others. Marx thinks that this stunts our growth. He thought, naively, that this would change under communism. We would no longer be forced into a single role. People would be freed from narrow social identities to do more what they want.

... man's own deed becomes an alien power opposed to him, which enslaves him instead of being controlled by him. For as soon as the division of labour comes into being, each man has a particular, exclusive sphere of activity, which is forced upon him and from which he cannot escape.[14]

Increasing specialism and division of labour, noted by Adam Smith, often combines with 'deskilling' and decreased work satisfaction. Work becomes drudgery.

Owing to the extensive use of machinery and to division of labour, the work of the proletarians has lost all individual character, and consequently, all charm for the workman. He becomes an appendage of the machine, and it is only the most simple, the most monotonous and the most easily acquired knack that is required of him.[15]

Marx could see around him how artisans (semi-independent small producers) were 'going under' and being turned into proletarians. Once-creative workers were being reduced to mere operatives or 'hands'. He assumes that we are creative beings who yearn to do something interesting and useful; and that we are social beings who find meaning and enjoyment through relating to others. He calls this need to be social and sociable our 'species-being' and claims that it is damaged by alienated labour conditions.

An immediate consequence of the fact that man is estranged from the product of his labour, from his life activity, from his species-being is the *estrangement of man* from *man*. When man confronts himself, he confronts the *other* man.[16]

Note how Marx connects what people make (the 'product of labour') with their 'life activity', their 'species-being' and how they feel towards each other (estrangement). For the purpose of analysis, we may separate all these out (and box them into different subjects), but for Marx the main thing is the links between what people do and how they are; and the gap between what people could be and how society actually is. Everyone is alienated, but the rich are at least at ease in their alienation.

> The propertied class and the class of the proletariat present the same human self-estrangement. But the former class feels at ease and strengthened in this self-estrangement, it recognises estrangement as its own power and has in it the semblance of a human existence. The latter feels annihilated in estrangement; it sees in it its own powerlessness and the reality of an inhuman existence.[17]

Other Explanations of Misery

There are, of course, other and probably better views of unhappiness:

> If we examine our lives we will probably discover that most of our time and energy is directed towards mundane aims such as seeking material and emotional security, enjoying the pleasures of the senses, or achieving a good reputation. Although these things can make us happy for a short time, they are not able to provide the deep and lasting contentment we long for. Sooner or later our happiness turns into dissatisfaction and we find ourselves engaged in the pursuit of more worldly pleasures. Directly or indirectly, worldly pleasures cause us mental and physical suffering by stimulating attachment, jealousy and frustration. Moreover, seeking to fulfil our own desires often brings us into conflict with others.
>
> If true fulfilment cannot be found in worldly pleasures, where can it be found? Happiness is a state of mind, therefore the real source of happiness lies in the mind, not in external conditions. If our mind is pure and peaceful we will be happy, regardless of external circumstances, but if it is impure and unpeaceful we will never find happiness, no matter how much we try to change our external conditions.[18]

The above passage emphasises what Marx neglected: the inner world. What the Buddhist view shares with Marx is the conviction that objects do not guarantee happiness, any more than money buys love. In this respect, they are both anti-consumerist: they imply that most commodities (things which are bought and sold), other than bare necessities such as food and shelter, do not increase happiness, however much advertisers claim otherwise. Through consumerism, we scratch an itch that can never be cured by more commodities. For the Buddhist, this is because happiness is a state of mind. For Marx, it is because humans are social beings who find fulfilment not through relating to commodities, but through relating to each other and through doing creative, truly productive work.

The Politics of Unhappiness

Marx was probably not attempting a full explanation of unhappiness, but rather to change the way we look at it. Usually we *psychologise* misery: we blame it on the individual, labelling them as depressive, or whatever. Instead of 'blaming the victim', Marx shows misery as a widespread social malaise, whose cause is the way we organise (or fail to organise) society. Marx *politicises* misery. The theory of alienation had to be vaguely plausible, but its main purpose was to show unhappiness as something shared and social. Its aim was to make mass misery a political issue.

More specifically, Marx took his vocabulary ('alienation' and 'self-estrangement') from contemporary philosophers. According to Hegel, spirit or Mind (*Geist* in German) has been alienated; and history is the process which reunifies it. As we develop as human beings, we make the world part of our self again, we *comprehend* it. Feuerbach argued that we 'alienate' our higher self and higher potential by projecting it on to an illusory divinity. Marx appropriates the term and gives it a radically new, social and political meaning. He transposes philosophical discourse into political discourse. For him, alienation is not something metaphysical (about the 'human predicament'), but a social phenomenon. He asks what are the social causes of why people project their own human power on to something external, some reified abstraction which comes to control them. And this leads him to analyse the worldly forms of alienation: in religion, in the State, in class society and exploitation.

Alienation and Late Marx

Marx's main writing on alienation as such is in the *Economic and Philosophic Manuscripts* of 1844. After that, he looked at alienation more in terms of exploitation and political economy. Even in 1845, he was writing that the alien power which enslaves people 'turns out to be the *world market*'.[19] In 1848, he criticises the 'German literati' who merely talk about 'Alienation of Humanity', instead of analysing 'the economic functions of money'.[20] Marx himself began to analyse the economic aspects of alienation: money, capital, work and exploitation. This is the work for which he became best known.

Most of Marx's writing on alienation – in the *Economic and Philosophic Manuscripts of 1844* – was not published until the 1930s. When it did appear, it initiated a debate about how this early 'humanist' Marx writing about alienation fits in with the later 'scientific' Marx writing about economics. Some suggested there are 'two Marxes', separated by an 'epistemological break', but in fact there is no absolute rupture. 'Early Marx' merges into 'late Marx'. The general idea of alienation recurs in Marx's later writing. Thus he notes that through science humans have greatly increased powers, but we do not use those powers constructively, for human fulfilment. Instead of making machines serve humanity, we are reduced to servants of the machine.

> At the same pace that mankind masters nature, man seems to become enslaved to other men or to his own infamy. Even the pure light of science seems unable to shine but on the dark background of ignorance. All our invention and progress seem to result in endowing material forces with intellectual life, and in stultifying human life into a material force.[21]

This failure to use science to abolish the evils of poverty and injustice was, Marx thought, due to an inhuman, 'alienated' way of organising society. 'Machinery is misused in order to transform the worker, from his very childhood, into a part of a specialised machine.'[22] Once again it is easy to see how his thought might apply to the Victorian age; the question is whether it still applies to ours.

Marx's later work analyses the forms (social, economic and political) which alienation takes in capitalist society. The basic idea of alienation is always close and is sometimes explicitly re-stated. Thus, in the *Grundrisse* Marx writes that 'the working individual *alienates* himself';

> ... he relates to the conditions brought out of him by his labour, not as to the conditions of *his own,* but of *alien wealth,* and of his own poverty.[23]

The extent to which the 'mature' Marx retained the idea of alienation can be demonstrated in purely quantitative terms. The index to the 1861–63 economic manuscripts (preparatory work for *Capital*) contains 57 references to alienation.[24] In a single reference, the word 'alien' (or 'alienated') appears 12 times over three pages.[25] On two pages which are not even entered under 'alienation' in the index, the word 'alien' appears 17 times.[26] It is often associated with the verb 'confront', which appears 12 times over these five pages. 'Alienation' is very much about confrontation, mutual antagonism, arising from '*a relationship imposed by force*'.[27]

Quite apart from these details of textual continuity, Marx retains the general idea of alienation in his wider thought and tries to specify its *particular* forms. Thus, instead of talking about alienation in the labour process, he speaks of 'complete de-individualisation of labour, confinement in barrack-like factories, military discipline, subjugation to the machinery, regulation by the stroke of the clock, surveillance by overseers, complete destruction of any development in mental or physical activity'.[28] He is describing a form of alienation without using the word. In his political writing, he kept the idea of alienation, though in a narrower sense than in his early work.

... the economical subjection of the man of labour to the monopoliser of the means of labour, that is, the sources of life, lies at the bottom of servitude in all its forms, of all social misery, mental degradation and political dependence.[29]

Alienation Now

Marx argued that we are alienated from:

* the means of production;
* the work process itself;
* the product of labour;
* fellow humans;
* our 'species-being';
* and the true sources of our creativity.

Alienation is about power exerted by class society and the very products which humans have made; and our subsequent lack of self-actualisation. Marx seems to have believed that alienation would increase steadily under capitalism and industrialisation, until it reached an intolerable point, at which moment it would be ended by workers' revolution, leading to emancipation. Perhaps alienation does increase with industrialisation, but then levels off and declines due to prosperity, more like a Bell curve on a graph, rather than a straight line.

Since Marx, the word 'alienation' has branched out to indicate a broad, psychosocial malaise. Ann Oakley wrote about the alienation of those housewives who feel trapped in institutionalised low-grade torture.[30] Children and students are alienated by an education restricted to grades and 'merely useful' knowledge, rather than 'really useful' knowledge and self-development. In the work-place our very personality can become the instrument of an alien purpose. The sales-force, secretaries and others put up a false front and mobilise their inner resources to maintain the facade, perhaps inducing stress-related diseases and a miserable denial of self. Then there is the special alienation of racism, where an out-group is alienated by the superiority and hostility of the dominant group.[31]

There have been attempts to reduce alienation at work, notably co-ops. The multi-skills work group, pioneered in Japan, decreases the amount of purely repetitive work and increases the scope for diversity, self-management and self-respect. It can be backed up by employee participation in the company culture and share options, to give the worker a stake in success. Away from the factory floor, public sector workers and other professionals could feel not alienated but fulfilled, if their product is a useful service providing job satisfaction and if they have some control over how they achieve goals.

Marx ultimately sees alienation in terms of class and who owns the means of production. It is probably better to consider this as just one axis of domination among others. Eco-activism is an example of a non-class based power struggle to overcome alienation. A full understanding of alienation would have to consider what Marx neglected, such as alienation from:

- feelings, intuition, spirituality and higher self;
- sense of community.

Alienation does not come only from capitalism, but from urbanisation too. Whether 'capitalist' or 'socialist', the city turns others into strangers, aliens, objects of suspicion. It is made for cars, which decreases the amount of home territory where children can play and the citizen feels safe. To reduce this kind of alienation it is necessary to revive a sense of community, support, security and trust: to understand what communities are; how they work best; and how they can be sustained and nourished. These are not issues of social class alone.

Questions

1. Is 'alienation' a product of Marx's imagination?
2. Is 'alienation' *intrinsically* connected with capitalism?
3. Does it make sense to see 'alienation' as a cause of crime?
4. Is the theory of alienation anything more than a museum piece for the history of ideas?
5. 'Alienation is a negative concept which encourages self-indulgent posturing and a morbid rejection of life.' Discuss.
6. What, if anything, can 'alienation' tell us about unhappiness?
7. 'Unhappiness is a state of mind.' Is it?
8. Which, if any, of the following are symptoms of alienation:
    - joy-riding;
    - a national lottery;
    - computer porn?
9. What are the root causes of alienation?

CHAPTER 4

How Marx (re)wrote History

This chapter

• shows how Marx re-wrote history;
• indicates some of the subjective aspects of his historical writing;
• illustrates these subjective aspects by detailed reference to one passage;
• suggests a good approach to reading Marx's work closely.

In Marx's time, most history was military, diplomatic and political history: the 'history of great men'. In contrast to this, Marx focused on the lives of ordinary people, especially working people.

Consider, by way of example, Marx's writing about Tudor England. Instead of describing the Spanish Armada, Sir Walter Raleigh and courtiers in ruffs, Marx gives a glimpse of life for the 'have-nots'. He is summarising the 'Act for the Punishment of Vagabonds', 1572.

> Elizabeth, 1572: Unlicensed beggars above 14 years of age are to be severely flogged and branded on the left ear unless someone will take them into service for two years; in case of a repetition of the offence, if they are over 18, they are to be executed, unless someone will take them into service for two years; but for the third offence they are to be executed without mercy as felons. Similar statutes: 18 Elizabeth, c. 13, and another of 1597.[1]

This was a law to harass the poor. Marx is no antiquarian, delving into past minutiae for their own sake. He is passionately interested in the lives of ordinary people; suffering and oppression; and showing the links between events in different parts of the world.

> The discovery of gold and silver in America, the extirpation, enslavement and entombment in mines of the aboriginal population, the beginning of the conquest and looting of the East Indies, the turning of Africa into a warren for the commercial hunting of black-skins, signalised the rosy dawn of the era of capitalist production. These idyllic proceedings are the chief momenta of primitive accumulation. On their heels treads the commercial war of the European nations, with the globe for a theatre. It begins with the revolt of the Netherlands

from Spain, assumes giant dimensions in England's anti-Jacobin war, and is still going on in the Opium Wars against China &c.[2]

Marx focuses on the mass suffering, genocide and extreme oppression often neglected in conventional histories. He is, typically, dealing with subjects about which most healthy humans would have strong feelings. He invokes an extreme reality which has all the extra force of one which has often been repressed. His irony ('rosy dawn' and 'idyllic proceedings') may be a way of both heightening the sense of outrage in the reader and suppressing it in himself.

His account could be described as humanist in that it concerns people – their lives and deaths. It is also structuralist in that it shows these people as dwarfed by a larger historical process (the 'primitive accumulation of capital'). The people are in a sense absent *as people*. The actual experience of natives and colonists is largely left to the imagination. Humans are only half-present as moral agents. Responsibility is displaced on to abstracts (such as 'capitalist production').

The first sentence echoes and recalls Hegel:

> These three events – the so-called Revival of Learning, the flourishing of the Fine Arts and the discovery of America and of the passage to India by the Cape – may be compared with that *blush of dawn*, which after long storms first betokens the return of a bright and glorious day.[3]

The allusion to Hegel is parody and pun, a refutation and a transformation, a correction and a homage. Marx, like Hegel, is describing the 'big picture', world history. His narrative has a sense of grandeur and drama, as it sweeps across the continents, spanning the centuries, as if it, like capitalism, has 'the globe for a theatre'.

Marx publicises wrong, but in locking it into his wider theory, he may allow the reader to dismiss the wrong, along with the theory, as mere propaganda. He does not dwell on suffering for its own sake, or merely to expose wrong-doing. He uses this suffering, this forgotten history, to bolster his argument. To some extent, he appropriates the oppression of others, for his own ends. If capitalism had deprived indigenous people of everything except their suffering, then Marx seized on that too, as the raw material for his own history.

Perhaps, however, we are extrapolating too much from too little. The longer extract below, taken from *Capital*, describes the 'gangs' of labourers who roamed the countryside looking for work in nineteenth-century Britain.[4] It is the kind of life described by Thomas Hardy and the passage is rather like a Victorian equivalent of the documentary, mixing description and analysis. Note, for example, the following:

- Marx's sources and references;
- his attitude to the various groups;
- his use of rhetoric, passion and irony,
- the emotions he deploys;
- the emotions he conceals;
- how much of the force of the argument – intellectual and moral – is conveyed in footnotes.

"The gang consists of from ten to forty or fifty persons, women, young persons of both sexes (13–18 years of age, although the boys are for the most part eliminated at the age of 13), and children of both sexes (6–13 years of age). At the head of the gang is the gang-master, always an ordinary agricultural labourer, and usually what is called a bad lot, a rake, unsteady, drunken, but with a dash of enterprise and *savoir faire*. He is the recruiting-sergeant for the gang, which works under him, not under the farmer. He generally negotiates with the latter over piece-work, and his income, which on the average is not very much above that of an ordinary agricultural labourer (a), depends almost entirely on the dexterity with which he manages to extract the greatest possible amount of labour from his gang within the shortest time. The farmers have discovered that women only work steadily under the direction of men, but that women and children, when once set going, spend their vital forces impetuously – as Fourier already knew in his time – whereas the adult male worker is shrewd enough to economize on his strength as much, as he can. The gang-master goes from one farm to another, and thus employs his gang for from six to eight months in the year. Employment by him is therefore much more lucrative and more certain for the labouring families than employment by the individual farmer, who only employs children occasionally. This circumstance so completely rivets his influence in the open villages that children can in general be hired only through his agency. The lending-out of the latter, individually and independently of the gang, is, a subsidiary trade for him.

The 'drawbacks' of this system are the over-working of the children and young persons, the enormous marches that they make every day to and from the farms, which are five, six and sometimes seven miles away, and finally, the demoralization of the 'gang'. Although the gang-master, who is called 'the driver' in some districts, is armed with a long stick, he seldom uses it, and complaints of brutal treatment are exceptional. He is a democratic emperor, or a kind of Pied Piper of Hamelin. He must therefore be popular with his subjects, and he binds them to himself by the charms of the gipsy life which flourishes under his auspices. Coarse freedom, noisy jollity and the obscenest kind of impertinence give attractions to the gang. Generally the gang-master pays up in a public house; then he returns home at the head of the procession of gang members, reeling drunk, and propped up on either side by a stalwart virago, while children and young persons bring up the rear boisterously, and singing mocking and bawdy songs. On the return journey – what Fourier calls *phanerogamie* (b) is the order of the day. Girls of 13 and 14 are commonly made pregnant by their male companions of the same age. The open villages, which supply the contingents for the gangs, become Sodoms and Gomorrahs (c), and have twice as high a rate of illegitimacy as the rest of the kingdom. The moral character of girls bred in these schools, when they become married women, was shown above. Their children, when opium does not finish them off entirely, are born recruits for the gang.

The gang, in its classical form, as we have just described it, is called the public, common or tramping gang. For there also exist private gangs. These are made up in the same way as the common gang, but count fewer members, and work, not under a gang-master, but under some old farm servant, whom the farmer does not know how to employ in any better way. The gipsy fun has vanished in this case, but, according to all the witnesses, the payment and treatment of the children is worse.

The gang-system, which has steadily expanded during the most recent years (d), clearly does not exist for the sake of the gang-master. It exists for the enrichment of the large-scale farmers (e) and indirectly for the land-owners (f). For the farmer, there is no more ingenious method of keeping his labourers well below the normal level, and yet of always having an extra hand ready for extra work, of extracting the greatest possible amount of labour with the least possible expenditure of money (g), and of making adult male labour redundant. From the foregoing expositions it will be understood why, on the one hand, a greater or lesser lack of employment for the agricultural labourer is admitted, while, on the other, the gang-system is at the same time declared necessary on account of the shortage of adult male labour and its migration to the towns (h). The cleanly weeded land and the unclean human weeds of Lincolnshire are pole and counterpole of capitalist production (i).

Marx's footnotes

(a) Some gang-masters, however, have worked up to the position of farmers of 500 acres, or proprietors of whole rows of houses.
(b) Charles Fourier, *Le Nouveau Monde Industriel et Sociétaire*, Paris, 1829, Part 5, Supplement to Chapter 36, and Part 6, Summary. Here Fourier describes 'phanerogamie' as a means of limiting the population. It is a form of polyandry practised within the phalanx, that is, the communal unit which was, to replace the family, and is compared explicitly by Fourier himself with the sexual behaviour of various tribes in Java and Tahiti.
(c) 'Half the girls of Ludford have been ruined by going out' (in gangs) (*Children's Employment Commission, Sixth Report*, Evidence, p. 6, n. 32).
(d) 'They' (the gangs) 'have greatly increased of late years. In some places they are said to have been introduced at comparatively late dates; in others where gangs ... have been known for many years ... more and younger children are employed in them'(ibid., p. 79, n. 174).
(e) 'Small, farmers never employ gangs.' 'It is not on poor land, but on land which affords rent of from 40 to 50 shillings, that women and children are employed in the greatest numbers' (ibid., pp. 17, 14).
(f) One of these gentlemen found the taste of his rents so delicious that he indignantly declared to the Commission of Inquiry that the whole hullabaloo was only due to the name of the system. If, instead of 'gang', it were to be called 'the Agricultural Juvenile Industrial Self-Supporting Association', everything would be all right.
(g) 'Gang work is cheaper than other work; that is why they are employed,' says a former gang-master (ibid., p. 17, n. 14). 'The gang-system is decidedly the cheapest for the farmer, and decidedly the worst for the children,' says a farmer (ibid., p. 16, n. 3).
(h) Undoubtedly much of the work now done by children in gangs used to be done by men and women. More men are out of work now where children and women are employed than formerly (ibid., p. 43, n. 202). On the other hand, 'the labour question, in some agricultural districts, particularly the arable, is becoming so serious in consequence of emigration, and the facility afforded by railways of getting to large towns that I' (the I in question is the steward of a great lord) 'think the services of children are most indispensable' (ibid., p. 80, n. 180). The 'labour question' in English agriculture districts, unlike, the rest of the civilized world, – means the 'landlords' and farmers' question', namely how, despite an always increasing exodus of

the agricultural folk, can a sufficient relative surplus population be kept up in the country, thereby keeping the wages of the agricultural labourer at a minimum?

(i) The *Public Health Report* already cited, in which the gang-system is treated in passing, in connection with the subject of the mortality of children, remains unknown to the press, and therefore, unknown to the English public. The last Report of the Children's Employment Commission, however, afforded the press sensational and welcome copy. While the Liberal press asked how the fine gentlemen and ladies, and well-paid clergy of the state Church, with whom Lincolnshire swarms, people who expressly send out missions to the antipodes 'for the improvement of the morals of South Sea Islanders' could allow such a system to arise on their estates, under their very eyes, the more refined newspapers confined themselves to reflections on the coarse degradation of an agricultural population which was capable of selling its children into such slavery! Under the accursed conditions to which these 'delicate' people condemn the agricultural labourer, it would not be surprising if he ate his own children. What is really wonderful is the healthy integrity of character he has largely retained ... ."

To illuminate the motives and dynamics of Marx's writing, consider his attitudes to the groups he describes.

The Gang Labourers

Marx's initial stance towards the gang labourers may seem quite distanced and objective. The people are quantified and categorised to show the composition of the gang. Implicitly, there is compassion for their plight, although this is not directly expressed. In the second paragraph, when noting the drunkenness of gang life, Marx expresses some horror, mixed with fascination, evident in the detail with which he fleshes out his description of how they are paid.

In describing the sexual life of the gang. Marx sounds both matter-of-fact and appalled. The villages are described as 'Sodoms and Gomorrahs'. We might ask whether Marx's appeal here to conventional Victorian morals is genuinely heartfelt; or how far it is a rhetorical ploy to manipulate the prejudices of his readers. When not sounding scandalised, Marx (footnote (b)) shows a sort of anthropological (dis)interest in the sexual practices of the gang, comparing it with the tribes in Java and Tahiti.

At the end of the passage, Marx calls the labourers 'unclean human weeds' – a stylistic joke, which also contains a trace of distaste and contempt?

The Gang-master

For the gang-master, Marx has disapproval, mixed with a dash of admiration. His contradictory attitude mirrors the contradictory position of the gang-master, whose income remains low, even though he exploits his work-force. In the second paragraph, the gang-master becomes a more magical, enchanting figure, 'a kind of Pied Piper of Hamelin' (which implicitly casts his labourers as errant children).

The Liberal Press

Marx approves of and enjoys how the liberal press has exposed the hypocrisy of the wealthy and the clergy (footnote (i)). He also shows scepticism about its sincerity, suggesting that the story was 'welcome and sensational copy'.

Missionaries

Marx has condemnation and contempt for the hypocrisy of preaching to South Sea Islanders, whilst ignoring poverty at home (footnote (i)). The tone is both angry and amused, a controlled vitriol. Marx's hostility to the missionaries is perhaps also born of fear: fear of their competing and still-dominant world-view.

The 'More Refined Newspapers'

The narrowness and meanness of the 'more refined newspapers' is clearly exposed (footnote (i)). Marx's language becomes more Latinate and pseudo-philosophical ('confined themselves to reflections on the coarse degradations'), possibly mimicking the orotund vacuity of 'refined' journalism. He condemns such papers for their lack of heart and lack of understanding, whilst also indicating that nothing else should be expected of them.

* * *

Marx's effects can be quite complex and ambiguous. Consider the sentence at the end of the second paragraph.

> Their children, when opium does not finish them off entirely, are born recruits for the gang.

The tone might variously be described as pitying, matter-of-fact or callous. The style is terse. Marx does not elaborate on the sufferings of the children (in the way that Dickens might have done). They are 'finished off' in a single sentence. The cynicism is perhaps both a mask and a rhetorical device. Lack of sentimentality enhances the status of the narrator (as 'objective', reliable and given, if anything, to understatement) and thus the impact of his account.

Marx never directly and openly releases the feelings behind his work. They are 'kept at the boil' and provide much of the persuasiveness and pressure of the narrative. Although Marx does not fully express the emotion, his work contains and sustains a powerful mixture of compassion, anguish and anger.

These various emotions are both deflected and heightened by irony. For instance, Marx devotes a footnote to the 'gentleman' who declared that 'the whole hullabaloo was only due to the name of the system. If, instead of gang, it were to be called "the Agricultural Juvenile Industrial Self-Supporting Association", everything would be all right' (footnote (f)). Humour is the shortest line between two people. The irony pays an implicit compliment to the reader's intelligence and lightens an otherwise grim passage. This keeps the reader sweet. The detail convinces in that it rings all too true. It aligns the reader with Marx as narrator, creating a compact, a shared feeling that 'we can see through these "gentlemen"'. Marx gets us on the same side as him. If we agree with his position here, as is likely, we are more likely to be won by his overall argument.

In sum, Marx's appeal to our emotions and values is central and integral to the project. It is also legitimate, given the subject. The paradox or anomaly is that at the level of theory, Marx almost systematically diverts our attention from his moral and emotional base. These factors are shunted off into the 'superstructure'.

How does Marx's account of gang labour relate to his wider theory of history? There are at least four quite loose connections.

1. Throughout the passage, Marx emphasises the class character of English agriculture as (a) capitalist and (b) class divided between landlord/tenant farmer/labourer.
2. Marx concentrates on the lives of working people and work conditions: their exploited relationship to their ultimate employer (the farmer) and their immediate manager (the gang-master). In terms of his theory, Marx is writing about *relations of production*.
3. He tries to show how these relations of production have changed and what has brought about the increase in child labour. His answer in this case (given briefly) is that the railways made it easier for the men to emigrate to large towns, so that farmers began to use more child labour instead. The railways are due to recent developments of steam power. In terms of Marx's theory, this has to do with the *forces of production*.

4. He is interested in how people (mis)represent reality to themselves, how they cushion themselves from hard facts with half-truths and self-deception. Thus he notes how 'the steward of a great lord' identifies with his master and pronounces that 'the services of children are most indispensable'(footnote (i)). With respect to Marx's theory, this is the realm of *ideology* and *false consciousness*.

As a generalisation, it is best to read Marx in a way that is both critical and constructive, with an eye to

- all he overlooks, the gaps and evasions, the silences and contradictions in his work;
- how he altered many of his ideas and predictions over time;
- how he mixes polemic and analysis;
- the interactions of intellectual, moral, emotional and imaginative elements in his writing.

Questions

1. Is it fair to accuse Marx of using descriptions of extreme suffering for his own political ends?
2. To what extent is it possible or even desirable to write history devoid of emotion and value judgements: a history that never takes sides?

CHAPTER 5

History According to Marx

This chapter

- explains the basic idea of the 'materialist conception of history';
- demonstrates the theory by two examples: (a) the collapse of the USSR and (b) Marx's own writing about the emergence of capitalism;
- analyses historical materialism in more detail and assesses it.

Historical Materialism: the Basics

Marx set out to explain what he saw around him: increased technology and increasing poverty. To analyse the causes of this, he asked historical questions of the largest kind:

- Why do things change?
- What are the patterns of change?
- Can we control change (for the better)?
- What is the role of the individual in change?

Marx's theory of history is known as the 'materialist conception of history', or historical materialism. It seeks to explain historical change by examining technological progress, social development and class struggle. As a first approximation, this is how the model looks:

politics + ideas: the state, law, the arts, religion (*ideology*)
SUPERSTRUCTURE
⇞⇞⇞⇞⇞⇞⇞⇞
society + economic structure (*relations of production*)
FOUNDATION
⇞⇞⇞⇞⇞⇞⇞⇞
science + technology + labour power (*forces of production*)
GROUND

Marx posits that one explains history by showing how developments in the base (forces of production) ultimately cause changes in the superstructure. At one level, historical materialism is *just that simple*.

In practical terms, it helped to encourage the study of 'ordinary life' – how people live and produce and exchange goods – not just extraordinary events.

Example 1. The USSR

Consider the collapse of the Soviet Union. It is easy to say what a historical materialist explanation would *not* involve. It would not explain events purely or even mainly by reference to a single individual (Mikhail Gorbachev, Boris Yeltsin or Ronald Reagan). Nor would it involve mystical interpretations, such as planetary conjunctions, collective karma or divine intervention.

A strict version of historical materialism might explain the collapse of state socialism in terms of new forces of production. New technologies (the microchip and personal computers) were incompatible with a top-heavy 'command' economy, a centralised bureaucracy and close control of information and production. In order to compete in global markets, the USSR needed a computer-literate population. This entailed a more open, modern society. Purely on technological and economic grounds, the old order had to go. The forces of production demanded changes in the relations of production – and that entailed a revolution in the political and ideological superstructure.

This is not a bad explanation and certainly better than reducing everything to the personality of Mikhail Gorbachev. But, once again, it is best to apply historical materialism in a creative way, by using Marx's general terms: technology, class interests, the market, profit, ideology and power.

The sudden collapse of state socialism should be related to longer-term processes. We might go back to the initial difficulty of establishing socialism in non-industrial, semi-feudal, Tsarist Russia; the traumatic birth pangs of the new regime; armies marching to 'strangle communism in its crib'; invasion from without and insurrection within; the massacre of the richer peasants (the kulaks); the famines of the 1920s; the massive industrialisation of the 1930s; the 'Great Purges' and the 'Great Patriotic War'; dislocation in the relations of production and the eventual failure of socialist ideology. Once the collective faith in socialism had sunk below a critical level, no motivation to work remained. Demoralisation set in.

This would set the scene for the sudden, dramatic fall of the Communist Party. State socialism no longer met the needs of the economy; economic growth had tailed off; the people were disillusioned. Part of the army clung on to the old ideology, which served to legitimise its sectional interest in a high military budget.

But a mixture of privileged bureaucrats and entrepreneurs stood to gain from a more capitalist system, which offered more opportunities for self-advancement than rigid socialism. To some extent they could ensure that popular dissatisfaction and complaints about corruption took a form and a course suitable to their own particular interests.

Thus, a study in 1994 by the Russian Institute of Sociology reported that former members of the party-state elite (the 'nomenklatura') make up 75 per cent of President Boris Yeltsin's new administration; 74 per cent of top Russian government officials; 83 per cent of regional leaders; 60 per cent of parliamentarians; and 41 per cent of the new business class.[1] Most of the new businessmen came from the middle levels of the former Soviet technical and managerial classes. While 17 per cent were former apparatchiks of the Soviet Young Communist League, only 5 per cent could be described as self-made. Women 'have been largely eliminated from the new elite'.

If fully fleshed out with this kind of empirical work, a creative application of Marx's method could offer a plausible account of the collapse of the USSR. We may wonder, however, whether such a wide-ranging explanation should still be called historical materialist; and whether historical materialism can account for important psychosocial phenomena in the collapse of communism: conformism and careerism, stagnation and sycophancy, complacency and corruption, mass militarisation and sexual repression.

Example 2. The Rise of Capitalism

To see how Marx himself applied his theory, consider his writings about the transition from feudalism to capitalism. He wanted to show how the world of nineteenth-century London (capitalism) had emerged from a world of barons and peasants (feudalism). To see why this might interest him, consider the passage below.

> Nature does not produce on the one hand owners of money or commodities, and on the other hand men possessing nothing but their own labour power. This relation has no basis in natural history, nor does it have a social basis common to all periods of human history. It is clearly the result of past historical development, the product of many economic revolutions, of the extinction of a whole series of older formations of social production.[2]

The emergence of capitalism interests Marx in the first instance because it transformed the lives of ordinary people. By studying it, he could show the historical origin of classes and of ideas. He could suggest that poverty and class society are not eternal and natural, but merely transitory products of an historical phase. In this way, his use of history links to his theory of ideology. He can show that ideas, including economic ones, are products of history.

In the *Communist Manifesto*, Marx explains the development of capitalism in line with his theory of historical materialism: the productive forces eventually developed to such a degree that feudalism became inappropriate, inefficient, irrational and even impossible.

> We see then: the means of production and of exchange, on whose foundation the bourgeoisie built itself up, were generated in feudal society. At a certain stage in the development of these means of production and of exchange, the conditions under which feudal society produced and exchanged, the feudal organisation of agriculture and manufacturing industry, in one word, the feudal relations of property became no longer compatible with the already developed productive forces; they became so many fetters. They had to be burst asunder; they were burst asunder.
>
> Into their place stepped free competition, accompanied by a social and political constitution adapted to it, and by the economical and political sway of the bourgeois class.[3]

This explanation accords with a strict interpretation of historical materialism (changes in the forces of production set off changes in the relations of production and the superstructure). But, as a historian, Marx also paints a more complex, composite canvas.

> From the serfs of the Middle Ages sprang the chartered burghers of the earliest towns. From these burgesses the first elements of the bourgeoisie were developed.
>
> The discovery of America, the rounding of the Cape, opened up fresh ground for the rising bourgeoisie. The East-Indian and Chinese markets, the colonisation of America, trade with the colonies, the increase in the means of exchange and in commodities generally, gave to commerce, to navigation, to industry, an impulse never before known, and thereby, to the revolutionary element in the tottering and feudal society, a rapid development.
>
> The feudal system of industry, under which industrial production was monopolised by closed guilds, now no longer sufficed for the growing wants of the new markets. The manufacturing system took its place. The guild-masters were pushed on one side by the manufacturing middle class; division of labour between the different corporate guilds vanished in the face of division of labour in each single workshop.

Meantime the markets kept ever growing, the demand ever rising. Even manufacture no longer sufficed. Thereupon, steam and machinery revolutionised industrial production. The place of manufacture was taken by the giant, Modern Industry, the place of the industrial middle class, by industrial millionaires, the leaders of whole industrial armies, the modern bourgeois.

Modern industry has established the world market, for which the discovery of America paved the way. This market has given an immense development to commerce, to navigation, to communication by land. This development has, in its turn, reacted on the extension of industry; and in proportion as industry, commerce, navigation, railways extended, in the same proportion the bourgeoisie developed, increased its capital, and pushed into the background every class handed down from the Middle Ages.

We see, therefore, how the modern bourgeoisie is itself the product of a long course of development, of a series of revolutions in the modes of production and of exchange.[4]

Marx goes on to outline other factors which helped push a feudal society into a capitalist one:

- 'the need of a constantly expanding market';
- 'new wants, requiring for their satisfaction the products of distant lands and climes';
- 'universal inter-dependence of nations';
- centralisation of population (in towns);
- concentration of property in a few hands;
- centralisation of the means of production (in factories);
- growth of the nation-state;
- development of the modern working class – 'a class of labourers who live only so long as they find work'.[5]

For capitalism to develop, a class of independent or semi-independent producers (such as peasants), who work for themselves and make enough to live on (and perhaps more besides), has to be turned into a class of wage labourers. The new wage labourers do not own their work-place, do not have enough land to subsist on and have no independent income. They therefore have to work for a capitalist employer.

Marx wants to analyse this change: to show how 'great masses of men are suddenly and forcibly torn from their means of subsistence, and hurled onto the labour-market as free, unprotected and rightless proletarians. The expropriation of the agricultural producer, of the peasant, from the soil is the basis of the whole process.'[6] His analysis goes well beyond a theory about technology influencing society.

In actual history, it is a notorious fact that conquest, enslavement, robbery, murder, in short, force, play the greatest part.[7]

Marx describes the violent process by which peasants were evicted from the land; how common land was 'enclosed' and turned into private property; and how arable land was turned into sheep pastures (which were more profitable and required fewer agricultural workers). He links the dispossession of the peasants to the expanding market for wool.

The rapid expansion of wool manufacture in Flanders and the corresponding rise in the price of wool in England provided the direct impulse for the evictions. The old nobility had been devoured by the great feudal wars. The new nobility was the child of its time, for which money was the power of all powers. Transformation of arable land into sheep-walks was therefore its slogan.[8]

In a sophisticated account of 'the revolution in the relations of production',[9] Marx examines much more than just technological development.

Feudal society, for its part, was destroyed by urban industry, trade and modern agriculture. (Even by some inventions, e.g. gun powder and the printing press.)[10]

The emergence of capitalism was also helped along by the dissolution of the monasteries.

The process of forcible expropriation of the people received a new and terrible impulse in the sixteenth century from the Reformation, and the consequent colossal spoliation of church property. The Catholic church was, at the time of the Reformation, the feudal proprietor of a great part of the soil of England. The dissolution of the monasteries, etc., hurled their inmates into the proletariat. The estates of the church were to a large extent given away to rapacious royal favourites, or sold at a nominal price to speculating farmers and townsmen, who drove out the old-established hereditary sub-tenants in great numbers, and threw their holdings together ... . The property of the church formed the religious bulwark of the old conditions of landed property. With its fall these conditions could no longer maintain their existence.[11]

Marx also mentions forced redundancy of feudal hangers-on;[12] the fall in the value of the precious metals; and the role of lowered wages and higher prices in strengthening 'a class of capitalist farmers'.[13] In practice, therefore, Marx uses historical materialism in a flexible, creative way, as a 'lever for study'. His account encompasses many factors. And he spells out the interactions of the various dynamics, not merely in the bland, anodyne abstractions of social theory, but 'in letters of blood and fire'.[14]

> The spoliation of the Church's property, the fraudulent alienation of the state domains, the theft of the common lands, the usurpation of feudal and clan property and its transformation into modern private property under circumstances of ruthless terrorism, all these things were just so many idyllic methods of primitive accumulation. They conquered the field for capitalist agriculture, incorporated the soil into capital, and created for the urban industries the necessary supplies of free and rightless proletarians.[15]

Marx was a practising historian, who was quite ready to stretch or transgress his theory if need be. There is a creative tension between his theory (which specifies an area of research, excludes extraneous factors and focuses awareness) and his actual historical work (which expands the area of research, embraces outside factors and broadens awareness). His wish for consistency and the neatest possible explanation clashes with his wish to be comprehensive and to offer the fullest possible explanation.

Marx's account of the transition from feudalism to capitalism is incomplete and imperfect. He disregards the importance of demographic factors – the population increase under way. And modern historians argue that the enclosures actually created more work than they destroyed. Marx mentions many factors which enabled or precipitated the transition from feudalism to capitalism, but he does not collate them into a single, unified account. He does not show precisely how the transition occurred; why it happened as it did; and why it was irreversible. The best explanation – one which Marx gestures towards – has to do with a notion of competitive primacy, or survival of the fittest.[16] A feudal society (already including some merchants, money-lenders and independent artisans) which allows pockets of capitalism to develop will reap benefits in terms of dynamism and innovation, for entrepreneurs will now have a strong motive to develop the forces of production. It will be better placed for trade and to develop new kinds of weapons, both of which give it a decisive competitive edge over a society which quashes its pockets of protocapitalism.

A 'Guiding Thread'

Marx's theory of history now needs to be examined more carefully. We begin with what he calls his 'guiding thread'. (Superscript letters denote later comments.)

In the social production of their existence, men[a] inevitably enter into definite[b] relations, which are independent of their will, namely relations of production appropriate to a given stage in the development of their material forces of production[c]. The totality of these relations of production[d] constitutes the economic structure[d] of society, the real foundation, on which arises a legal and political superstructure[e] and to which correspond definite[b] forms of social consciousness. The mode of production of material life conditions[f] the general process of social, political and intellectual life. It is not the consciousness of men that determines[f] their existence, but their social existence that determines[f] their consciousness. At a certain[b] stage of development, the material productive forces of society come into conflict with the existing relations of production, or – this merely expresses the same thing in legal terms – with the property relations within the framework of which they have operated hitherto. From forms of development of the productive forces these relations turn into their fetters. Then begins an era of social revolution. The changes in the economic foundation lead sooner or later to the transformation of the whole immense superstructure.[17]

The passage needs careful reading. Note the following:

(a) Marx is saying that in life and especially at work, we are forced, willingly or not, into various roles and relationships. We have to take our place in a social structure which we have not ourselves chosen.

Marx is probably using 'men' in the generic sense. We may nonetheless ask: what of women's history? (Or children's?) Marx focuses on the public sphere of production, which, especially in Victorian times, was a 'man's world'. Can his method illuminate the 'private' world, the 'sphere of reproduction'?

(b) The adjective 'definite' is part of an idiom of certainty. It suggests a degree of precision and predictability which may not actually be there.[18]

(c) The 'forces of production' refer to the forces of science and technology. More precisely, the forces of production consist of (i) the means of production: tools, machinery, premises, raw materials; and (ii) labour power: strength of producers, skills, technical knowledge.

The productive forces tend to develop, as human ingenuity confronts the challenges of scarcity.[19]

(d) Marx is saying that, like it or not, we are caught up in a web of relations, to do with work and production. These 'relations of production' may be defined as power relations over people and/or productive resources: relationships of ownership, authority and control, over workers and their skills, monetary assets, raw materials, land, buildings, machines and even scientific knowledge.

Marx's 'economic structure' includes property relations, income distribution, employees' contracts, etc. Where he says 'economic' we might say 'socioeconomic'. He even suggests that 'force is the midwife of every society which is pregnant with a new one. It is itself an economic power.'[20]

(e) Marx is using a metaphor of a building: foundation (= economy, etc.) and superstructure (= ideology, etc.).

Metaphors open theoretical questions, rather than settling issues. This one may be interpreted in several ways. Although it emphasises the foundations (economic), it need not follow that the rest (the 'superstructure') is merely passive. Roofs stabilise pillars on which they rest. One foundation may support various kinds of superstructure and the whole purpose and function of a building *is* the superstructure. Marx's theory must itself be part of the superstructure and necessarily limited by the (nineteenth-century) foundation from which it arose.

(f) The English 'conditions' and 'determines' (with its connotations of determinism) translate two German words, *bestimmt* and *bedingt,* of which the second could be translated as 'condition' or 'influence'. To say that social factors *influence* our thinking is much more plausible than to say that they *determine it.*[21]

Problems

If the idea of examining the interactions of technological, economic and social factors now seems common sense, that in itself is testimony to Marx's success. A commentator today need not be a card-carrying historical materialist, any more than a scientist need be a card-carrying Newtonian. In its time, historical materialism was a revolutionary insight, a way of accounting for historical change, without reference to God or some repeated, cyclical pattern.

Marx's theory raises several problems.

1. The Problem of Primacy

There appears to be a contradiction between the role of class struggle and the productive forces. Which comes first? Which instigates social change? Historical materialism posits the primacy of the productive forces, but elsewhere Marx emphasises class struggle, most famously at the start of the *Communist Manifesto*.

> The history of all hitherto existing society is the history of class struggles.

The apparent contradiction may be resolved by saying that social groups deal with conflict between forces and relations of production *through class struggle*. Class struggle is (chief) among the 'forms in which men become conscious of this conflict and fight it out'.[22]

Another solution would be to say that the problem of primacy is like the chicken and the egg. It is a non-problem. Since in practice neither can appear without the other, it is merely scholasticism to make an absolute theoretical distinction. Marx said to remember the

> *Dialectic of the concepts productive power (*means of production*)*
> *and relation of production,* a dialectic whose limits have to be defined and which does not abolish real difference.[23]

The idea of a dialectic suggests a two-way process, a perpetual interaction, reciprocal causation. The question of primacy may thereby be solved (or shelved).

2. *The Problem of Determinism*

With God thrown out of history, some of the traditional problems of theology – concerning free will and predestination – resurfaced in secular, philosophical form. Theologians had puzzled: 'are life, fate and history predestined by God?'. Marx reframed the problem as: 'are life, fate and history pre-decided by socioeconomic factors?'. He had already broached this question, at a personal level, aged 17.

> But we cannot always attain the position to which we believe we are called: our relations in society have to some extent already begun to be established before we are in a position to determine them.[24]

The problem is to know what role is left for human agency if we are really bound by the 'iron necessity' of 'the natural laws of capitalist production'.[25] There are two main solutions to this. The first is to read historical materialism as an off-shoot of Marx's theory of alienation. It refers only to history in an alienated society – what Marx sometimes called pre-history. Our alienation consists of being bound by laws beyond our ken and control. The whole point then is to transcend those laws. As Marx puts it, in a typical chiasmus, we face 'the task of replacing the domination of circumstances and of chance over individuals by the domination of individuals over chance and circumstances'.[26]

A second solution is to posit a two-way process, or dialectic, between the individual and social change. People are 'both the authors and the actors of their own drama'.[27] 'Circumstances make men just as much as men make circumstances.'[28]

Men make their own history, but they do not make it just as they please; they do not make it under circumstances chosen by themselves, but under circumstances directly encountered, given and transmitted from the past. The tradition of all the dead generations weighs like a nightmare on the brain of the living.[29]

Society grows out of production, but also affects production. It is, once again, a two-way process. (Superscript letters refer to notes on pp. 42–3.)

The specific[b] economic form, in which unpaid surplus-labour is pumped out of direct producers, determines[f] the relationship of rulers and ruled, as it grows directly out of production itself *and, in turn, reacts upon it as a determining[f] element* .... It is always the direct relationship of the owners of production to the producers – a relation always naturally corresponding to a definite[b] stage in the development of the methods of labour and thereby its social productivity – which reveals the innermost secret, the hidden basis of the entire social structure, and with it the political form of the relation of sovereignty and dependence, in short, the corresponding specific[b] form of the state.[30]

Marx adds that 'the same economic base', affected by 'innumerable different empirical circumstances, natural environment, racial relations, external historical influences etc.' will show 'infinite variations and gradations in appearance, which can be ascertained only by analysis of the empirically given circumstances'. This relatively subtle exposition can take into account many different variables.

Historical materialism was sometimes 'vulgarised' into a dogma that history is just the working out of economic laws. An equal and opposite error was to ascribe change merely to key individuals. This perhaps sprang from a paradox implicit in Marx's theory. Would not the Marxist leader, who 'scientifically' understands the dynamics of history, be furnished with the historical power to transcend those laws of history? Lenin and Stalin, who both propounded a narrow interpretation of historical materialism, were themselves glorified *as individuals* in a cult of personality. The official 'Marxist' histories of officially Marxist states seldom analysed their revolutions in terms of discrepancies between the forces of production and the relations of production. Instead they emphasised the glorious role of the leader: Lenin, Mao or Castro. The individual, reduced by the materialist conception of history, returns magnified as Hero of the People.

3. The Problem of Teleology

Marx, it is said, thought that History was advancing to a certain goal (a *telos* in Greek). He was guilty of teleology, setting up a linear History, a belief in the inevitability of proletarian revolution.

> It is not a question of what this or that proletarian, or even the whole proletariat, at the moment regards as its aim. It is a question of what the proletariat is, and what, in accordance with this being, it will historically be compelled to do.[31]

Marx could properly be condemned here for teleology (as well as dogmatism and wishful thinking). But then, 60 pages later, he is explicitly anti-teleological.

> *History* does *nothing*, it 'possesses *no* immense wealth', it 'wages *no* battles'. It is *man*, real, living man who does all that, who possesses and fights; 'history' is not, as it were, a person apart, using man as a means to achieve *its own* aims; history is *nothing but* the activity of man pursuing his aims.[32]

Some of Marx's proclivity for teleology may derive from Hegel, who saw history as the development of the Absolute Mind (*Geist*) from a state of alienation to one of full self-consciousness. In the Hegelian grand design, history is developing to a point at which alienation will be progressively overcome and the many (facts) will be triumphantly reconciled with the one (*Geist*). Marx sees history as leading to the triumph not of *Geist* but of the proletariat, or socialised humanity. But his conviction that capitalism would give way to a 'higher phase' is not just about teleology; it has more to do with optimism, faith and maintaining morale. At other times, he foresaw two alternatives, 'socialism or barbarism': either 'a revolutionary reconstitution of society at large' or 'the common ruin of the contending classes'.[33]

4. The Problem of Precision

Broad categories such as class and ideology can abet lazy, over-generalised explanations. To say for instance that X occurs because it is in the interests of the ruling class, may be true, but is never adequate. We have to show more exactly how and why X occurs; who is involved; what their interests are; and *exactly how* they influence X.

To put this in more technical terms, Marxism too easily slips into a sloppy mix of 'methodological holism' (explanations in terms of large groups or classes) and 'functional explanation' (citing the consequences of X in order to account for X). It ignores the actual behaviour of individuals, the 'micro-foundations' of explanation.

It does not specify feedback loops or the causative mechanisms which convert micro-motives into macro-behaviour.[34] The challenge is to apply theoretical concepts to specific instances, not just to use them as slogans and banners and master-keys.

Assessment

There are several different versions of historical materialism, from the loose to the strict. In the loosest sense, Marx is maintaining that 'life determines consciousness', that the production of the necessities of life is the basis for the production of ideas. This is a theory only in the loosest sense: a vantage point, a way of looking at things, a useful perspective, which focuses history on to everyday life, rather than military heroics. But there is also a stricter theory, a model or set of propositions about 'base' and 'superstructure' and the relations between them. Marx's writing has a tension between these two kinds of theory. As a theoretician he favours something quite precise, but as a historian, he wields his ideas more freely. It is an untidy but productive combination.

Historical materialism presents itself as logical – even 'scientific'. The validity of this claim has been much debated. In particular, some critics (Analytical Marxists) have tried to make Marx live up to the dictates of 'hard' theory, expecting his work to meet the highest standards of internal coherence and to fulfil the most exacting (mathematical) criteria for consistency. Irrespective of whether this is an appropriate demand, it runs the risk of neglecting all the other things – rhetorical, emotional, moral, imaginative – which Marx is doing with his theory. In these other dimensions, mathematical consistency counts for little. There is no reason to suppose that the interaction or articulation of these other dimensions should be able to be formalised in a consistent, codifiable way. The emotional, moral and literary ('extra-logical') dimensions which do much to constitute Marx's history coincide and interact with each other, simultaneously and interdependently. They elude systematisation.

Marx himself cautioned against 'employing the all-purpose formula of a general historico-philosophical theory'.

> ... events strikingly analogous, but occurring in different historical milieus, led to quite disparate results. By studying each of these evolutions on its own, and then comparing them, one will easily discover the key to the phenomenon, but it will never be arrived at by employing the all-purpose formula of a general historico-philosophical theory whose supreme virtue consists in being supra-historical.[35]

What Marx called his materialist conception of history is best understood as a set of creative hypotheses, a manifesto, a research agenda that is validated or vindicated by the work it inspired. It is, in Engels' words, 'above all a guide to study'.[36] It provided a framework and a method; a set of values, assumptions, perspectives and priorities: a paradigm.[37] It gave a new emphasis to the historical role of the forces of production and to the centrality of relations of production. It foregrounded the interaction of technology, science, economic and social factors. Like any theory of history this involved a gamble, a simplification, a neglect of some areas. The gamble paid off in that Marx gave more impetus to new research and debate – especially in social and economic history and popular culture – than has any other historian, then or since. He did not write the definitive history of anything, but he did pioneer field after field for new enquiry.

Questions

1. a) Give a *brief* summary of Marx's materialist conception of history.
   b) What are the best aspects of Marx's approach?
   c) What are its main limitations?
2. Did Marx have a unified, coherent theory of history, or just a set of creative hypotheses?
3. 'The best explanation for the political failure of Marxism is a historical materialist one.' Discuss.
4. Use the 'materialist theory of history' in a creative way to explain any one event from recent history.
5. If, as Marx wrote (1847), 'the hand-mill gives you society with the feudal lord; the steam-mill, society with the industrial capitalist', what do the micro-chip and modern technologies give you?
6. To what extent could historical materialism reveal the causes behind any *one* of the following:

   • the destruction of rain forests;
   • the end of apartheid;
   • the decline of the House of Windsor.

CHAPTER 6

Class and Society

This chapter

- describes Marx's ideas about the main different kinds of society – the main 'modes of production';
- lists the 'contradictions of capitalism';
- shows how Marx adapted his theory of class in practice;
- assesses the usefulness of his ideas and the accuracy of his predictions.

Everyday Notions of Class

In countries where people are often thought to be especially 'class conscious', social class is usually taken to involve a whole range of personal factors – lifestyle, wealth, culture, accent, attitudes, education and 'breeding'. Here is a list prepared by a British target-marketing company. It classifies people according to their shopping and leisure behaviour, which reflects family background, values, self-image, etc.

1. Golf clubs and Volvos
2. The got set
3. Bon viveurs
4. Fast trackers
5. The high techs
6. Faith, hope and charity
7. Safe, steady and sensible
8. Craftsmen and homemakers
9. Trinkets and treasures
10. Cultural travellers
11. Carry on camping
12. Health and humanities
13. Wildlife trustees
14. Factories, fishing and football
15. Lager, crisps and videos
16. Instant chic
17. Gardeners' Question Time
18. Pools, horses and pubs
19. Survivors
20. Reading, religion and routine.[1]

Non-Marxist sociologists, stemming from Weber, are a little more systematic, focusing above all on a person's occupation, which is thought to be one of the main determinants of lifestyle, income, social status, connections and marketable skills. People may then be classified as below:

A Higher professionals
B Managerial and Technical
C1 Skilled non-manual
C2 Skilled manual
D Semi-skilled
E Unskilled

This kind of stratification helps to account for differences in social behaviour, life chances, health, etc.

Marx on Class

Marx's view of social class is not completely at odds with these conventional and sociological views. But unlike them his descriptions of class are always bound up with an explanation of general social structure and historical change. Thus, in his view, each phase of historical evolution has its own characteristic class structure – or 'mode of production' – and its own tendency to change in particular ways.

The main 'modes of production' are:

1. 'primitive communism', hunter-gatherer tribes, perhaps with some simple agriculture;
2. Graeco-Roman slave states;
3. feudalism;
4. capitalism;
5. socialism, which divides into a 'lower phase' and a 'higher phase'.[2]

Each mode of production has its distinctive class structure. Thus feudalism has the King, the barons, the Church and the peasants. Capitalism has:

- the big land-owners, aristocracy, nobility; can be seen as a residual class from feudalism, increasingly supplanted by the bourgeoisie;
- the bourgeoisie: owners of the factories (means of production), the transport system (means of distribution) and the big shops (means of exchange). Marx distinguishes between industrial capitalists (for example mill-owners) and finance capitalists (the 'bankocracy');

- the petty bourgeoisie: small-scale businesses, shopkeepers, etc. In times of boom, they aspire to the bourgeoisie. In recession, they shift towards the proletariat;
- the proletariat: those who have nothing to sell but their labour-power. The worker 'belongs not to this or that capitalist, but to the capitalist class, and it is his business to dispose of himself, that is to find a purchaser within this capitalist class';[3]
- the lumpen proletariat: 'the "dangerous class", the social scum, that passively rotting mass thrown off by the lowest layers of old society'.[4] This is what is now called the under-class: criminals, beggars etc.

Capitalism exists when the wealth-creating enterprises are privately owned by the few (the bourgeoisie) and most people have to sell their labour-power and work for the bourgeois. It is especially important to Marx because it is the type of society in which he lived and which he hoped would change, partly under his influence, into a better form of socialist society. Its two key classes, which decide its future, are the bourgeoisie and the proletariat.

In the *Manifesto of the Communist Party*, Marx claimed that capitalism had simplified the class antagonisms. 'Society as a whole is more and more splitting up into two great hostile camps, into two great classes directly facing each other: Bourgeoisie and Proletariat.' In his later work, he mentions 'middle and transitional levels' and 'the infinite fragmentation of interests and positions into which the division of social labour splits not only workers but also capitalists and land-owners'.[5] He notes

the constantly growing number of the middle classes, those who stand between the WORKMAN on the one hand and the capitalist and LANDLORD on the other. The middle classes maintain themselves to an ever increasing extent directly out of REVENUE, they are a burden weighing heavily on the WORKING base and increase the social security and power of the UPPER TEN THOUSAND.[6]

Marx also recognises that a judicious measure of upward mobility can stabilise society. It 'reinforces the rule of capital itself, widens its basis and enables it to recruit ever new forces from the lower strata of society ... . The more a dominant class is able to absorb the best people from the dominated classes, the more solid and dangerous is its rule.'[7] But Marx fails to integrate this awareness into his wider vision of revolution and social change.

Marx defines classes according to whether they own the means of production, or not. For him, class is about the transfer of surplus from below and the exercise of power from above. Classes are 'based upon *economic* conditions independent of their own will, and are forced into the most virulent contradictions by these conditions'.[8] He examines how people's lives are objectively related to power structures, especially control of the means of production, in the belief that this would show how people would line up in a revolutionary crisis.

With some exceptions, Marxist sociologists have concentrated on the traditional working class (in heavy industry), rather than analysing the middle classes and the growth of transnational ruling classes.[9] They have tried to develop and clarify the concept of class by tabulating the degree to which members of each class can expect to control

- the means of production (land, factories, etc.);
- money, capital or investments;
- their work setting;
- whether or how to sell their labour power;
- choice of school, training and how to spend time.

One useful idea to arise from this is 'contradictory class location'. Imagine a rising star in the civil service. According to Marx's theory at its crudest, she is a proletarian, because she still has to sell her labour-power. But, because she owns some investments and shares, as well as a pension, which give her an indirect stake in the means of production, she is also petty-bourgeois. Her education gives her some degree of choice over where and when to work; her job allows some control over investment decisions and work setting; and her pay gives her status and choice of holidays. Her family and friends and their own job security or lack of it may also tug her loyalties in different directions. The concept of 'contradictory class location' suggests the conflicting interests and impulses at work in a person.

The 'Contradictions of Capitalism'

Society develops, in Marx's view, as a result of technological change and class struggle, both of which set up tensions or contradictions. Several contradictions are especially prominent within capitalism:

- Factories and research labs need to maximise profit, to head off competition. They innovate or they go under. Science and technology are always advancing and this change sets off social changes. So we live in an ever-changing world. But the ruling classes also want stability, to enjoy their riches. The purpose of ideology, it has been said, is to stabilise society. There is a 'contradiction' between the *dynamic nature of the forces of production* and the *stabilising function of the ideological superstructure.*

- The interests of the *owners* contradict those of the *workers*. The owners always want to maximise *profit* at the expense of wages; the workers want to maximise *wages* at the expense of profit.

- There is a contradiction between *giant monopolies* and multinationals which can control much of the production process and *small business*, which often gets squeezed out of the market.

- There is a pattern of *boom* and *slump*. When the economy is swinging, capitalists want to borrow money, expand output and maximise profit. Eventually, the market is glutted, goods don't sell, confidence sags and a recession starts, with cutbacks and lay-offs. Then the whole wasteful process recommences. This is called the 'tendency to overproduction'.

- There is a *'tendency for the rate of profit to fall'*. Capitalists are always looking to introduce new technology to cut costs. But, according to Marx and the 'labour theory of value', profit ultimately derives from labour performed by workers ('variable capital'). The increase in machinery ('constant capital') means that in the long run the rate of profit will fall (although, Marx adds, this may be off-set by other factors).[10]

- A tension exists between the *short-term* aim of each capitalist to maximise profit; and the *long-term* needs of capitalist society to tax profit and invest in education, research, physical infrastructure, etc.

- There is a contradiction between the needs of capitalism (maximum *profit*, efficiency, survival of the fittest businesses) and *real human needs* (leisure, self-development, fun). This is the contradiction Marx explored in his theory of 'alienation'.

There are at least two further contradictions, for modern times.

- First, there is the contradiction of mass advertising, or the contradiction between increasing demand and increasing *expectations*. In seeking to increase market demand through images of slick, state-of-the-art goods and the life beautiful, capitalism cannot help but increase demands for a higher standard of living. False expectations created by advertising may lead to chronic dissatisfaction or rioting.

- Second is the contradiction between the ideal *consumer* and a sustainable *environment*. Capitalists have to sell as much as possible as fast as possible, to maximise profit and beat competitors. Newspapers, for example, compete to publish the most lurid and steamy news. Mass consumerism leads to environmental destruction and ecological crisis. Put another way, it would be a capitalist's dream to persuade every Chinese family that they needed two cars, a fridge and a holiday in Spain – but the environmental consequences would be horrendous. The interests of profit are often opposed to those of the environment.[11]

Marx's Theory in Practice

In analysing the events of his day, Marx adapts and refines his theory of class. Consider, for instance, 'The Class Struggles in France, 1848 to 1850'. Here Marx distinguishes between two main factions of the bourgeoisie:

(a) the 'industrial bourgeoisie', divided into 'reigning princes of the manufacturing interests', middle industrialists and smaller industrialists;[12]
(b) the 'finance aristocracy' or 'bankocracy'. This includes 'bankers, stock-exchange kings, railway kings, owners of coal and iron mines and forests, a part of the landed proprietors associated with them'.[13]

These two factions, along with the big land-owners, form the ruling class. In Marx's view, the finance aristocracy had the upper hand. It 'made the laws, was at the head of the administration of the state, had command of all the organised public authorities, dominated public opinion through the actual state of affairs and through the press'.[14] It had a direct interest in maintaining the state deficit, making extortionate loans to the state and speculating on the stock market. The bankers and their associates could precipitate 'sudden, extraordinary fluctuations in the quotations of government securities, the result of which was always bound to be the ruin of a mass of smaller capitalists and the fabulously rapid enrichment of the big gamblers'.[15] The industrial bourgeoisie was opposed to this instability and to the corruption of the finance aristocracy. Only fear of revolution pushed the industrial capitalist to ally with the stock exchange aristocracy. 'The reduction of his *profit* by finance, *what is that compared with the abolition of profit by the proletariat?*'[16]

Marx also distinguishes between the Paris proletariat, which can wield real power and influence at the centre of the political arena, and workers in the rest of France, 'crowded into separate, scattered industrial centres, being almost lost in the superior numbers of peasants and petty bourgeois'.[17]

Standing between the bourgeoisie and proletariat, is 'the mass of the nation, the peasants and petty bourgeois'. Peasants were 'the large majority of the French people'.[18] Their small-holdings are either owned or mortgaged. Their main enemy is the money-lender, who extracts interest on the mortgage for their land. The petty bourgeoisie includes 'keepers of cafés and restaurants, *marchands de vin* [wine merchants], small traders, shopkeepers, handicraftsmen, etc.'.[19] Finally there is the 'lumpenproletariat', 'a recruiting ground for thieves and criminals of all kinds, living on the crumbs of society'.[20]

Classes have their own interests and fears. They choose representatives, make alliances and compromises. Their struggles take many forms: economic measures, taxes, laws, decrees, elections, demonstrations, symbolic actions. The 'malcontent intermediate classes of French society' play a decisive role.[21] There is a role too for illusions and misconceptions. For example, Louis Napoleon can pose as a representative of the peasants. 'Just because he was nothing, he could represent everything save himself.'[22] Similarly, the Whigs in England could exploit and neutralise the impetus of the Reform movement. 'Each time they had taken the movement in hand in order to prevent its forward march, and to recover their own posts at the same time.'[23]

Assessment

Marx once assessed his achievement this way.

> Now as for myself, I do not claim to have discovered either the existence of classes in modern society or the struggle between them. Long before me, bourgeois historians had described the historical development of this struggle between the classes, as had bourgeois economists their economic anatomy. My own contribution was 1. to show that the *existence of classes is* merely bound up with *certain historical phases in the development of production;* 2. that the class struggle necessarily leads to the *dictatorship of the proletariat;* 3. that this dictatorship itself constitutes no more than a transition to the *abolition of all classes* and to a *classless society.*[24]

This is to claim both too much and too little. In particular, the second and third 'contributions' listed amount to little, except wishful thinking. Marx's lasting contribution is the way in which he

- describes the historical development of classes;
- relates society to technology, economics and ideology.

If the relations of production (society) derive from the forces of production, then the key issue becomes: who controls technology? Here Marx's analysis falters. Its defects emerge. For his predictions of social change are not based on any close or detailed empirical study. Rather, they stem from a general overview of history and society; a pattern of one class succeeding another; and a heavy dose of optimism.

Technological revolution has brought workers to power, but skilled, educated, professional workers: graduates, bureaucrats and technocrats. It has devolved power to these, but it has not destroyed capitalism or private ownership of the means of production. History seems to have proved Marx wrong in at least two key respects:

1. Society has not divided up into two great camps: bourgeoisie and proletariat. Instead of this polarisation, there has been a rise of the middle class: managers and professionals, in both public and private sectors, skilled, non-manual workers and technicians. There is some social mobility and the spectre, at least, of a meritocracy. (A Marxist might reply: 'In that they have to sell their labour power, what we call the "middle classes" are, in Marx's terms, actually proletarian.')

2. The workers have become richer, not poorer. The 'embourgeoisment' of the workers has occurred, not their 'immiseration' or 'pauperisation'. (The Marxist replies: 'But on the world scale, there is a widening chasm between rich and poor, "North" and "South".')

Pure capitalism would involve a completely 'free' market; profit before people; and survival of the fittest in a 'dog-eat-dog' world. However, we do not now live under pure capitalism, for the following reasons:

- *Monopolies* distort or even take over the 'free market'. Many goods and services require such a huge outlay that no individual enterprise could challenge the huge monopolies which produce or run them.
- *State ownership* operates in key areas of industry, such as transport systems.
- *State regulation* bridles capitalism by numerous laws, designed to protect the environment and prevent the worst excesses of profit-seeking.
- *Trade unions* and the *welfare state* ensure that wages are not cut down to the bare minimum.
- *Imperialism*. According to later Marxists, notably Lenin, capitalism has given way to imperialism. The profits from the home country are supplemented by 'super-profits' from abroad. Multinational enterprises, based in the 'imperialist' countries, exploit cheap labour and cheap raw materials in the 'Third World'.[25]

So modern capitalism might also be called:

- state capitalism;
- state monopoly capitalism;

- imperialism;
- neo-colonialism.

Later sociologists have suggested that we are now in a 'post-capitalist' society, characterised by increased affluence, full employment, a welfare state, less social division ('convergent strata') and a managerial revolution in which those who own industry do not necessarily control it – managers do instead.

Marx underestimates the importance of divisions *within* the working class, due to nation, region, gender, age, physique, ability, religion, etc. In emphasising class rather than nationalism, he was in fact being more *traditional* than we might suppose. For this was the accepted view of the aristocracy, who generally identified with their class equivalents abroad more than with their social inferiors at home. (Perhaps they still do.) Nationalism was then a middle-class creed, a way of taking power away from the aristocracy in the name of 'the people' and 'the country'.[26]

Marx had assumed that much of society's wealth would be squandered on private servants for the rich. He overlooks the possibility that:

- it could go instead to public servants, doing useful jobs for society – as nurses, teachers, school caretakers and dinner ladies, home helps, swimming bath attendants, play group leaders, etc.;
- ordinary people, a combination of working and middle class, could wield enough political clout to build and maintain a welfare society (financed by taxes, rates and the earnings of some nationalised industries) without going all the way to full, public ownership;
- capitalism could adapt to crises and even be strengthened by them.

That said, the age of welfarism and class compromise (in 'advanced industrial economies') may be cut short by:

- the continued globalisation of capitalism;
- increased competition (between Europe, the USA and the 'tiger economies' of the Pacific Rim);
- the predominance of 'supply side economics', which seeks to free up the factors of production and is thus anti-union, anti-regulation, anti-taxation and anti-welfare.

Countries with low wages, low taxes and minimal welfare may well undercut and out-compete high tax, welfare states. Moreover, in an age of electronic money, a government can no longer fund welfare through punitive taxes on the rich, who can easily move their funds off-shore. At the risk of sounding apocalyptic, it seems

that the social conditions which gave rise to Marx in the first place
could be returning, no doubt altered, perhaps with a vengeance.
If so, his analysis of capitalism and class could stage a come-back.

Questions about Class

1. What is gained by categorising individuals according to class?
   What is lost?
2. To what extent are most people's opportunities decided by
   birth and class?
3. Is there less class division than 50 years ago? Is there less than
   20 years ago?
4. What does it mean to be working class?
5. What would a classless society involve?
6. 'Social classes are large groups of people differing from each
   other (i) by the place they occupy in a historically determined
   system of social production, (ii) by their relation (in most
   cases fixed and formulated in law) to the Means of Production,
   (iii) by their role in the social organisation of labour and,
   consequently, (iv) by the dimensions of social wealth of which
   they dispose and (v) the mode of acquiring it. Classes are (vi)
   groups of people one of which can appropriate the labour of
   another owing to the different places they occupy in a definite
   system of social economy' (Lenin, 'A Great Beginning'). Is this
   a useful definition of class?
7. 'The working man respects the bourgeoisie, and wants to be
   a bourgeois' (G.B. Shaw). Is this true?
8. 'Marx forgets that the rich have often worked hard and deserve
   their success.' Discuss.
9. Does it make sense still to speak of 'the ruling class'? Or is it
   better to think in terms of social mobility, multiple centres of
   power, elites and 'leadership groups'?
10. Which matters more: class division or nationalism?

Questions about Society

1. 'The "contradictions of capitalism" is a resonant phrase, but
   in practice it refers only to tensions which can be solved – and
   in large measure have been solved – by judicious management
   and good governance.' Discuss.
2. Is it correct to say that society changes as a result of
   contradictions? If so, what are the main contradictions
   currently generating change? If not, what does cause social
   change?

3. 'Socialism is the painful road to capitalism.' What, if anything, is likely to be the next social stage after capitalism?
4. 'If Marx was a sociologist, he was one of an erratic and clumsy kind.' Discuss.
5. What would a purely capitalist society consist of? What would a purely socialist society consist of? How do these pure abstractions differ from actually existing societies?
6. 'There are many different varieties of capitalism. Marx's mistake was to lump them all together.' Discuss.
7. 'Some inequality is a small price to pay for efficiency, organisation and prosperity.' Is this adequate justification for capitalism?

CHAPTER 7

The Politics of Revolution

This chapter briefly sketches the political background to Marx's ideas and his opinions about other socialist groups. It then describes in more detail the development of his own ideas about revolution.

A Radical Tradition

A revolutionary tradition existed long before Karl Marx. In England alone, in the 50 years or so before he became a communist, there were many currents of popular radicalism: Jacobinism during and after the French Revolution; then Luddism (the destruction of machinery) and a time of 'revolutionary underground'. After the Napoleonic Wars, there was a fresh period of populist agitation; and then battles about trade unionism, freedom of the press, the Poor Law, the Factory Acts and electoral reform, up to the early 1830s. This was followed by the era of Owenism and Chartism. The scope and significance of these movements is hard to assess. Historians tend to look at events and actions; but if we focus instead on inaction, inertia and acceptance, then a different picture emerges.

Marx's Idea of Revolutionary Socialism

Marx and Engels were quick to dismiss such socialism as already existed. In the *Communist Manifesto* they attack the following varieties of socialism which existed in their time:

- 'feudal socialism': aristocrats using sympathy for the workers to denounce the bourgeoisie;
- 'clerical socialism': mere conscience-salving;
- 'petty-bourgeois socialism': nostalgic, unrealistic and ultimately reactionary;
- 'true socialism': (speaks of Humanity in general, supposes itself above class struggle);
- 'bourgeois socialism': do-gooders trying to stabilise bourgeois society, who want merely administrative reforms, not revolution;

- 'critical-utopian socialism' (Saint-Simon, Fourier, Owen): makes fantastic blue-prints for the future; then appeals to reason and society as a whole, especially the ruling class.[1]

Marx sharply differentiated his ideas of socialism from those of his contemporaries. In contrast to the Utopians, his socialism would be based on the actual march of history and the rise of the working class. He was against 'writing recipes for the cookshops of the future'.[2] Unlike Proudhon and Blanc, revolution would not involve mere reorganisation of credit and labour, but the full-scale abolition of class society. And whereas the conspirator Blanqui put his trust in a small cadre of revolutionists, Marx would rely on the mass organisation of the working class.

Influenced by Hegel's writing about contradiction, Marx thought that the 'contradictions of capitalism' would ensure its transformation. On one side was the state, described as 'the form in which the individuals of a ruling class assert their common interests',[3] an 'engine of class despotism', or 'the national war-engine of capital against labour'.[4] On the other, the main agent of change was the mass of the people, the working class.

> Economic conditions had first transformed the mass of the people of the country into workers. The domination of capital has created for this mass a common situation, common interests. The mass is thus already a class as against capital, but not yet for itself. In the struggle ... this mass becomes united, and constitutes itself as a class for itself. The interests it defends become class interests.[5]

The workers would come to realise their common interests through uniting in trade unions – 'bulwarks for the workers in their struggles with the employers'.[6] These would move from local grievances – stoppages, strikes and economic issues around the work-place – to dealing with larger, political questions.

> Trades unions work well as centres of resistance against the encroachments of capital. They fail partially from an injudicious use of their power. They fail generally from limiting themselves to a guerrilla war against the effects of the existing system, instead of simultaneously trying to change it, instead of using their organised forces as a lever for the final emancipation of the working class, that is to say, the ultimate abolition of the wages system.[7]

'The most advanced and resolute section of the working class', according to Marx, were the communists, owing to their internationalist and realist outlook.[8] They start out from 'actual relations springing from an existing class struggle'. The needs of the workers (increased wages) clash with the interests of the employer (profit). Workers, helped by improved means of communication, 'club together in order to keep up the rate of wages'.[9] Moreover, the ruling class has to educate and politicise the workers in order to compete with foreign manufacturers. In relying on its work-force it produces 'its own gravediggers'.[10]

After the defeat of the revolutions of 1848, Marx, exiled in London, remained defiant and set about reorganising the Communist League.

> For us the issue cannot be the alteration of private property but only its annihilation, not the smoothing over of class antagonisms but the abolition of classes, not the improvement of existing society but the foundation of a new one.[11]

The workers must not be contaminated by the 'democratic petty bourgeois'. During the struggle they should lead 'instances of popular revenge against hated individuals or public buildings', but also restrain 'the intoxication of victory' by 'a calm and dispassionate estimate of the situation and by unconcealed mistrust in the new government'. They should form their own municipal committees or workers' clubs and 'be armed and organised'.[12] The big feudal estates of the land-owners were to be confiscated and the workers

> must demand that the confiscated feudal property remain state property and be converted into workers' colonies cultivated by the associated rural proletariat with all the advantages of large-scale agriculture, through which the principle of common property immediately obtains a firm basis in the midst of the tottering bourgeois property relations.[13]

The workers should always outstrip the demands of the democrats 'and transform them into direct attacks upon private property'. The battle cry was 'Permanent Revolution'.[14]

By the end of 1850 Marx had come to think that a new outbreak of revolutions would depend on an economic crisis.

> *A new revolution is possible only in consequence of a new crisis. It is, however, just as certain as this crisis.*[15]

He was vague about how long this might take.

> ... we say to the workers: 'You will have to go through 15, 20, 50 years of civil wars and national struggles not only to bring about a change in society but also to change yourselves, and prepare yourselves for the exercise of political power ...'.[16]

No clues about what it would involve 'to change yourselves'.

In the 1850s Marx devoted his time to writing newspaper articles and his research in the British Museum Library. Then, in 1864, he again stepped up his political activity, to become the main light behind the new International Workingmen's Association – the First International. Marx described it as 'a real organisation of the working class for struggle',[17] 'the international counter-organisation of labour against the cosmopolitan conspiracy of capital'.[18] But the International was divided. The English trade union leaders wanted only reform; the French were influenced by Proudhon; and the Germans by Lassalle. From 1868, the anarchist ideas of Bakunin gained ground. Marx tried to negotiate and get his own way. Here he is talking about a programme he had written for the London delegates.

> I deliberately confined it to points which allow direct agreement and combination of efforts by the workers, and give direct sustenance and impetus to the requirements of the class struggle and the organisation of the workers into a class.[19]

Asked whether the International had a centralised form of government, Marx denied it and said 'the real form is designedly that which gives the greatest play to local energy and independence'.[20] It was 'a bond of union rather than a controlling force'. This was aspiration rather than fact, for the problem of organising in a way that is simultaneously empowering, democratic, flexible and effective remains unsolved. Marx himself was not immune to the seductions of power: he confided to Engels that 'when the next revolution comes ... we (i.e. you and I) will have this mighty ENGINE at our disposal'.[21]

The high point of the First International was the Paris Commune of 1871, which Marx hailed as a prototype of socialism, a real working-class government. But with the annihilation of the Commune, the International collapsed in a turmoil of in-fighting. Followers of the anarchist Bakunin tried to take over, so Marx had the headquarters moved to New York, where, as he surely anticipated, the organisation soon expired.

Marx's attention now switched to Germany. Banned from living there himself, he tried to maintain influence through his follower, Wilhelm Liebknecht. The foremost socialist, Ferdinand Lassalle, successful, charismatic and a brilliant orator, had been killed duelling in 1864. His followers and Liebknecht's group negotiated a common programme at Gotha, in 1875. Marx thought that this made too many concessions to the Lassalleans and wrote his *Critique of the Gotha Programme*.

In 1879, Marx and Engels re-emphasised the importance of class struggle. In the first sentence below, there may be an unusual hint of resignation or fatalism, as if they felt that in this matter they had only one honourable option.

As for ourselves, there is, considering all our antecedents, only one course open to us. For almost 40 years we have emphasised that the class struggle is the immediate motive force of history and, in particular, that the class struggle between bourgeoisie and proletariat is the great lever of modern social revolution; hence we cannot possibly co-operate with men who seek to eliminate that class struggle from the movement. At the founding of the International we expressly formulated the battle cry: The emancipation of the working class must be achieved by the working class itself.[22] Hence we cannot co-operate with men who say openly that the workers are too uneducated to emancipate themselves, and must first be emancipated from above by philanthropic members of the upper and lower middle classes.[23]

By this time, Marx was looking to Russia and Germany as the best candidates for revolution and seeing a long haul. Revolution is 'a mere stage on the road'.[24] Engels, at the end of his life, echoed this view; 'a revolution is a lengthy process'.[25] He believed that in Germany at least, the workers' party (the Social Democrats), who commanded 25 per cent of the vote, should continue to work through parliamentary means.

The two million voters whom they send to the ballot box, together with the young men and women who stand behind them as non-voters, form the most numerous, the most compact mass, the decisive 'shock force' of the proletarian army ... . The irony of world history turns everything upside down. We, the 'revolutionaries', the 'overthrowers' – we are thriving far better on legal methods than on illegal methods and overthrow.[26]

One other legal method praised by Marx was the co-operative movement. The value of co-ops, he wrote, 'cannot be over-rated'. Their one fault lay in being too modest and they 'ought to be developed to national dimensions'.[27]

Assessment

Marx saw revolutions as 'the locomotives of history',[28] but he always had two very different concepts in mind. One has to do with continued revolutionary advances in the forces of production, precipitating changes in society and in our thinking. This fairly open-ended forecast was certainly accurate. Since the technological revolution is happening anyway, and will lead to social change in the fullness of time, this kind of prediction makes no great call on the individual and can even foster a sense of Olympian detachment and confidence.

Marx also makes a more specific prediction about the nature of social change: that is, that it will inaugurate a communist society. This narrower, political conception of revolution has not on the whole been vindicated. It implicitly demands that the individual take sides, creating a sense of urgent, impassioned commitment, as if the moment of truth is nigh.

Political revolution comes in two main kinds. One is a whole social class effortlessly taking over. 'No revolution', Marx once said, 'can be made by a party'; it would 'be made by the majority'.[29] On other occasions, however, he clearly is thinking of a political party seizing power in a *putsch* or coup d'état. This introduces the problem of violence, a problem which Marx tended to side-step. He recognised that 'force must be the lever of our revolutions', although he allowed that there are countries, such as America, England and perhaps Holland, 'where the workers may achieve their aims by peaceful means'.[30] It is too easy though to have a glib formula – 'force must be the lever of our revolutions' – which evades and obscures the reality of suppressing resistance: the reality of prisons, re-education camps and all the problems unleashed by creating a punitive bureaucracy with special powers for monitoring, neutralising or crushing renegades. The neat recipe conceals a failure of the imagination.

Marx's general view is that capitalism impoverishes workers and this will drive them to revolution. He apparently forgets that being driven to desperation is not the same as being driven to revolution. Poverty breeds selfishness and self-hatred, not just solidarity. It can demoralise and depoliticise, as it does for the 'lumpen' down-and-outs. To some extent Marx realises this, as when he recognises the importance of the battle to limit the working day.[31] But, on the whole, he neglects the possibility that rising standards of living could help the workers to power, just as increased prosperity had furthered the rise of the bourgeoisie.

Overall, Marx's optimism about the prospects for socialist revolution is remarkable, especially given his awareness of the daunting obstacles.

> Competition separates individuals from one another, not only the bourgeois but still more the workers, in spite of the fact that it brings them together. Hence it is a long time before these individuals can unite ... .[32]

If competition divides workers more than it does the bourgeoisie, then the prospects for working-class unity are poor. Moreover, in his historical writing and journalism, Marx appreciates the importance of class coalitions among the rulers. For instance he notes the alliance in England between the big land-owners and the bourgeoisie, two classes finding themselves 'in perfect harmony'.

> On the one hand, the landed proprietors provided the industrial bourgeoisie with the labour force necessary to operate its manufactories and, on the other, were in a position to develop agriculture in accordance with the level of industry and trade. Hence their common interests with the bourgeoisie; hence their alliance with it.[33]

Marx notes that the British bourgeois 'prefer to compromise with the vanishing opponent [the aristocracy] rather than to strengthen the arising enemy [the working class]'.[34] Again, writing about the emancipation of the Russian serfs, he notes that class alliances against the oppressed are the norm: 'an understanding, as is usual in such transactions, has been arrived at between the existing powers at the cost of the oppressed class'.[35] But in his optimistic, revolutionary predictions, he overlooks this. He disregards the possibility that

(a) the 'ruling class' would ally or even merge with a class of highly educated technocrats and professionals, as well as incorporating other groups, to become the effective ruler of society – whether in name it is 'capitalist' or 'socialist';
(b) powerful media, rather than uniting the workers, could be used to divert and divide them;
(c) the go-getting dynamism of capitalism could be harnessed and channelled by society and combined with welfare institutions;
(d) society could control capitalism, rather than the other way round.

Questions

1. *Should* Marx have foreseen that his ideas could lead to Stalin's gulags?
2. Assess the adequacy of Marx's theory of the transition from capitalism to socialism.
3. Are Marx's ideas about revolution and socialism anything more than wishful thinking dressed up as serious theory?
4. Does the mass of people have any progressive role to play in history?

CHAPTER 8

Socialism and Communism

This chapter
- explains what Marx had in mind by communism;
- describes his enthusiasm for the Paris Commune;
- shows how he avoided writing about some of the practical problems communism would create.

Communism, According to Marx

Capitalism, Marx thought, was a necessary stage on the road to socialism, necessary in order to create a great increase in science and technology ('productive power') and a world market. It created the preconditions for communism which 'is only possible as the act of the dominant peoples "all at once" and simultaneously'.[1] This is, of course, just the opposite of what Stalin later called 'socialism in one country'.

The demand to abolish 'private property' does not refer to individual possessions, such as socks, spectacles or toothbrushes. It refers only to 'that kind of property which exploits wage labour':[2] the property of landlords and factory owners, those who own the instruments of production.

> Communism deprives no man of the power to appropriate the products of society; all that it does is to deprive him of the power to subjugate the labour of others by means of such appropriation.[3]

This is to be achieved by the 'formation of the proletariat into a class, overthrow of the bourgeois supremacy, conquest of political power by the proletariat'. The aim then would be, in the words of the *Manifesto*, to

- widen, to enrich, to promote the existence of the labourer;
- stop the exploitation of children by their parents;
- rescue education from the influence of the ruling class;
- do away with the status of women as mere instruments of production;
- abolish countries and nationality;
- put an end to the exploitation of one nation by another.[4]

67

The first step was 'to raise the proletariat to the position of ruling class, to win the battle of democracy'. The State would cease to be the arm of the landed classes and become 'the proletariat organised as the ruling class'.[5] Marx lists the kind of measures which might then be in order.

1. Abolition of all property in land and application of all rents of land to public purposes.
2. A heavy progressive or graduated income tax.
3. Abolition of all rights of inheritance.
4. Confiscation of the property of all emigrants and rebels.
5. Centralisation of credit in the hands of the State, by means of a national bank with State capital and an exclusive monopoly.
6. Centralisation of the means of communication and transport in the hands of the State.
7. Extension of factories and means of production owned by the State; the bringing into cultivation of wastelands, and the improvement of the soil generally in accordance with a common plan.
8. Equal liability of all to labour. Establishment of industrial armies, especially for agriculture.
9. Combination of agriculture with manufacturing industries; gradual abolition of the distinction between town and country, by a more equable distribution of the population over the country.
10. Free education for all children in public schools. Abolition of children's factory labour in its present form. Combination of education with industrial production, &c., &c.[6]

These are specific proposals, some of which have since been enacted, in 'capitalist' states as well as 'socialist' ones.

Marx had originally (1844) introduced communism in portentous terms, as a solution to a philosophical problem, as

the *genuine* resolution of the conflict between man and nature and between man and man – the true resolution of the strife between existence and essence, between objectification and self-confirmation, between freedom and necessity, between the individual and the species. Communism is the riddle of history solved, and it knows itself to be the solution.[7]

Later in life, he remained as reluctant as any fortune-teller to specify precisely what he was predicting. He cannily left his readers to fill in the details in their own imagination.

What we are dealing with here is a communist society, not as it has *developed* on its own foundations, but on the contrary, just as it *emerges* from capitalist society, which is thus in every respect, economically, morally and intellectually, still stamped with the birth marks of the old society from whose womb it emerges.[8]

Marx calls this 'the first phase of communist society' and he acknowledges its imperfections. People would be paid, not according to need, but according to contribution – the work they have put in.

But one man is superior to another physically or mentally and so supplies more labour in the same time, or can work for a longer time ... . Besides, one worker is married, another not; one has more children than another, etc. etc. Thus, given an equal amount of work done, and hence an equal share in the social consumption fund, one will in fact receive more than another, one will be richer than another, etc. ... these defects are inevitable in the first phase of communist society as it is when it has just emerged after prolonged birth pangs from capitalist society.

Having acknowledged these problems, Marx looks beyond them to 'a higher phase of communist society', where society is developed enough to 'inscribe on its banners: From each according to his abilities, to each according to his needs!'[9]

Lenin called the 'first phase of communist society' socialism and the 'higher phase' communism. This is a convenient short-hand, but Marx himself uses the terms almost interchangeably, to refer to a society of common ownership and production for use: or an end to the exchange economy (buying and selling), classes and the state. Although Marx lambasted the imprecision of the Gotha programme, there is a fateful ambiguity in some of his own formulations.

Between capitalist and communist society lies the period of the revolutionary transformation of one into the other. Corresponding to this is also a political transition period in which the state can be nothing but *the revolutionary dictatorship of the proletariat.*[10]

The resonant phrase 'dictatorship of the proletariat' now sounds like a paradox, or even oxymoron, in that 'dictatorship' suggests a minority, whereas 'proletariat' suggests the mass.[11] But, at the time, the word 'dictatorship' did not have its sinister, modern sense of anti-democratic authoritarianism. It referred merely to a breach of the constitution, perhaps even in the interests of democracy. Lenin took the phrase to mean a dictatorship by the Party (the advance guard of the working class) on behalf of the people. Marx may have meant something more democratic, something like 'people power'. But if so, he did not specify it and he thus opened the door to the Bolshevik interpretation. As time passed, an ideal of government by the people for the people gave way to a reality of government by the party for the party.

Marx sees communism in terms of collective responsibility, in terms which presage what ecologists now call sustainability and stewardship.

> From the standpoint of a higher socio-economic formation, the private property of particular individuals in the earth will appear just as absurd as the private property of one man in other men. Even an entire society, a nation, or all simultaneously existing societies taken together, are not the owners of the earth. They are simply its possessors, its beneficiaries, and have to bequeath it in an improved state to succeeding generations, as *boni patres familias* [good heads of the household].[12]

Communism involves nationalisation of the land and centralisation of the means of production.[13] Somehow – Marx does not say quite how – this leads to an association of free men, relations between whom are 'transparent in their simplicity'.[14] People are freed from narrow specialisms. 'In a communist society there are no painters but only people who engage in painting among other activities.'[15] There is no need for money either, though once again Marx is utterly vague about details: who will be in charge, what power issues will arise, etc.

> With collective production, money capital is dispensed with. The society distributes labour-power and means of production between the various branches of industry. There is no reason why the producers should not receive paper tokens permitting them to withdraw an amount corresponding to their labour time from the social consumption stocks. But these tokens are not money; they do not circulate.[16]

One way to get a more precise idea of what Marx envisaged is to consider his writings about the Paris Commune (1871), which he saw as the prototype of 'working-class government'.

The Paris Commune

In *The Civil War in France*, which appeared just after the defeat and slaughter of the Communards (1871), Marx especially praised the following features of the Commune:

* municipal councillors, chosen by universal suffrage;
* those elected responsible to the people and revocable at short term;

- these councillors to be a working body, 'executive and legislative at the same time' (this does away with an unelected, inaccessible and elitist Civil Service);
- 'the public service had to be done at workmen's wages';
- police to be 'responsible and at all times revocable';
- suppression of the standing army and the police;
- 'disestablishment and disendowment of all churches as proprietary bodies';
- priests return to private life, 'in imitation of their predecessors, the Apostles';
- education made accessible to all;
- 'Like the rest of public servants, magistrates and judges were to be elective, responsible and revocable';
- centralised government would 'give way to the self-government of the producers';
- 'the Commune was to be the political form of even the smallest country hamlet';
- 'destruction of the State power';
- makes 'cheap government a reality, by destroying the two greatest sources of expenditure – the standing army and State functionarism';
- abolishes monarchy, the 'indispensable cloak of class rule';
- 'abolition of the nightwork of journeymen bakers';
- 'prohibition, under penalty, of the employers' practice to reduce wages by levying upon their work-people fines under manifold pretexts';
- 'surrender, to associations of workmen, under reserve of compensation, of all closed workshops and factories', where the capitalist had absconded or locked workers out;
- did not 'pretend to infallibility, the invariable attribute of all governments of the old stamp';
- 'it published its doings and sayings, it initiated the public into all its shortcomings'.

For Marx, the Commune was supremely democratic since (in theory at least) the people could choose and recall their representatives, just as a boss hires and fires employees.

> Instead of deciding once in three or six years which member of the ruling class was to misrepresent the people in Parliament, universal suffrage was to serve the people, constituted in Communes, as individual suffrage serves every other employer in the search for the workmen and managers in his business. And it is well known that companies, like individuals, in matters of real business generally know how to put the right man in the right place, and, if they for once make a mistake, to redress it promptly.[17]

This would safeguard against self-seeking careerism. The difference of course is that 'the people' are not really analogous to a company, however large. Their interests are more diverse and conflicting and it is far harder for them to arrive at and maintain a state of consensus.

Marx praises the decentralising ideal of the Commune, although it is not clear whether this praise is sincere or merely tactical, since, in the *Communist Manifesto*, he had envisaged a highly centralised state. What Marx most liked about the Commune was its intention, its promise and the fact that it was 'a working-class government' – and one with some connection (however slight) to his own organisation.

> Its true secret was this. It was essentially a working-class government, the produce of the struggle of the producing against the appropriating class, the political form at last discovered under which to work out the economic emancipation of labour .... . Yes, gentlemen, the Commune intended to abolish that class-property which makes the labour of the many the wealth of the few. It aimed at the expropriation of the expropriators.[18]

By the end of his life, Marx had changed his tone and he described the Commune as 'merely an uprising of one city in exceptional circumstances', adding that most of the Commune

> was in no wise socialist, nor could it have been. With a modicum of COMMON SENSE, it could, however, have obtained the utmost that was then obtainable – a compromise with Versailles [its opponents] beneficial to the people as a whole.[19]

Assessment

Marx was certain that 'the blind rule of the supply and demand laws which form the political economy of the middle class' would give way to 'social production controlled by social foresight',[20] but this raises the host of problems which eventually sank the Soviet-style command economies. What exactly does 'social' mean in the phrase 'social production'? Who precisely will oversee it? Who will supervise supply and predict demand? What role will be left for the self-adjusting market?

An artful and habitual vagueness about the future state helps Marx to avoid discussing the problems socialism would face. He neglected practical matters such as how to:

- keep the spirit of revolution alive;
- let people really take charge of their own lives;
- provide incentives to work;

- deal with 'free riders' and idlers;
- ensure the necessary community spirit;
- handle resistance and protest;
- run the economy on democratic lines;
- replace the market as a means of distributing resources;
- have the necessary experts and specialists;
- stop administrators from becoming the new rulers;
- prevent the rhetoric of socialism being used as a cover for other interests.

The last oversight is perhaps a surprising one, because Marx, with his theory of ideology, was keenly aware how people and classes *use* ideas for their own ends. He did not apparently realise how successfully a caste of bureaucrats could employ his own ideas and ideals for *its* advantage. He had noted the dangers of bureaucracy early in his work, in the early 1840s.

> Bureaucracy is a circle from which no one can escape. Its hierarchy is a hierarchy of knowledge. The apex entrusts the lower circles with insight into the individual while the lower circles leave insight into the universal to the apex, so they deceive each other reciprocally ... .
>
> As far as the individual bureaucrat is concerned, the aim of the state becomes his private aim, in the form of a race for higher posts, of careerism.[21]

Marx made little of this insight at the time. Later, in 1851, he was to write vividly of the bureaucracy in France and its political role:

> This executive power with its enormous bureaucratic and military organisation, with its extensive and artificial state machinery, with a host of officials numbering half a million, besides an army of another half million, this appalling parasitic body, which enmeshes the body of French society like a net and chokes all its pores, sprang up in the days of the absolute monarchy, with the decay of the feudal system, which it helped to hasten.[22]

Again in 1871, his analysis of the civil war in France took into account 'the huge governmental parasite, entoiling the social body like a boa constrictor in the ubiquitous meshes of its bureaucracy, police, standing army, clergy and magistrature'.[23] His instinct was to smash the boa constrictor, not 'to transfer the bureaucratic-military machine from one hand to another, but to break it'.[24] Few constructive ideas about a replacement.

Other people did foresee that a 'socialist' bureaucracy could become a new tyranny. A former associate of Marx, Arnold Ruge, wrote that revolutionary socialism would install 'a police and slave state'.[25] Engels lamented that 'unfortunately it appears to be a law of the proletarian movement that everywhere a part of the workers' leaders necessarily become corrupted ...'.[26] The leading anarchist, Mikhail Bakunin, predicted a 'despotism of the *ruling minority*'. He saw socialism not as the antithesis of capitalism, but as a malign intensification of it. Once the workers become representatives of the people, he argued, they cease to be workers. 'So the result is the control of the vast majority of the people by a privileged minority.' The ex-workers 'will no longer represent the people, but only themselves and their "claims" to govern the people'. Marx gave this warning short shrift.

> If Mr. Bakunin were familiar even with the position of a manager in a workers' co-operative factory, all his fantasies about domination would go to the devil. He should have asked himself: what forms could management functions assume within such a workers' state, if he wants to call it that?[27]

In the light of history, the scorn is as misplaced as the optimism is unrealistic.

Questions

1. 'From each according to ability, to each according to need!' What would it take to make this a reality?
2. What are the main practical problems a socialist society faces?
3. Could socialism be 'marketed' in an attractive and convincing way? If so, how? If not, why not?
4. 'The Soviet Union was *not* communist, or even socialist, in Marx's sense of the words. But it *was* the logical outcome of trying to put Marx's ideas into practice.' Discuss.
5. What is bureaucracy? How does it spread? How is it best kept in check?
6. Could social ownership be combined with efficiency? If so, how? If not, why not?
7. Does socialism require intervention, coercion and repression?
8. Are Marx's ideas about revolution and socialism anything more than wishful thinking dressed up as serious theory?

CHAPTER 9

Ideology

This chapter

- discusses the connection between ideas and society;
- explains what Marx had in mind by 'ideology';
- indicates how his notion of ideology has been developed.

What Marx Meant by 'Ideology'

'Ideology' refers to the complex relationship between ideas and society: between the mind and sociocultural environment.

Marx sees ideas as being rooted in and growing from reality. Ideas affect society and society affects ideas. The two co-exist and interact. It is a two-way process – a dialectic.

Theory for Marx is neither neutral nor innocent. It is closely bound up with life and power relations in class society. He emphasises that ideas are influenced by the way society is organised, how we get food and shelter, how we produce and distribute goods, the material 'mode of production'.

> ... men, developing their material production and their material intercourse, alter, along with this their actual world, also their thinking and the products of their thinking. It is not consciousness that determines life, but life that determines consciousness.[1]

To some extent, this view is now taken as 'common sense'. So too is its corollary. Advertisers and politicians know that people from different social groups tend to think differently – to have different dreams and aspirations, etc. – and they fashion their message accordingly. We accept that people and their ways of thinking are to a considerable extent sociological phenomena.

Marx thought that most ideas – and especially those taught in schools and universities – support an oppressive status quo.

> The ideas of the ruling class are in every epoch the ruling ideas: i.e., the class which is the ruling *material force* of society is at the same time its ruling *intellectual* force. The class which has the means of material production at its disposal, consequently also controls the means of mental production, so that the ideas of those who lack the means of mental production are on the

whole subject to it ... . The individuals composing the ruling
class ... rule also as thinkers, as producers of ideas, and regulate
the production and distribution of the ideas of their age: thus
their ideas are the ruling ideas of the epoch.[2]

Marx concluded that although academics might see themselves
as sublimely above class struggle, they tended to be servants of the
State, 'sophists and sycophants of the ruling classes'.[3] Ruling class
ideology presents the status quo as natural, even eternal. This
'false consciousness' may spread to the workers too.

> The advance of capitalist production develops a working class
> which by education, tradition and habit looks upon the
> requirements of that mode of production as self-evident,
> natural laws.[4]

Ideology is what blinds the workers to the injustice of
exploitation. Its perpetrators include what Marx calls 'vulgar
economists' who go around 'proclaiming for everlasting truths, the
banal and complacent notions held by the bourgeois agents of
production about their own world, which is to them the best
possible one'.[5] In opposition to them, Marx wanted to analyse the
laws of 'bourgeois economy' to reveal 'a past lying behind
this system'.[6]

His aim was to challenge ideas which supported injustice; and
to create a new set of ideas (ideology) for liberation. He wanted
ideas to prepare workers for struggle. A simple example may
illustrate this. A firm meets increased competition and decides to
freeze wages, sack workers and increase the workload. Workers
armed with nothing more than common sense may be surprised
or shocked; they may blame it all on an evil boss, a crazy
government or their own rotten luck. They will moan, but they will
knuckle under. Marx wanted his theories – of philosophy, history,
economics and politics – to explain events; show their place in the
bigger pattern; indicate what was likely to happen next; and reveal
how it could all be improved. The activist in him wanted ideas to
empower people, not to intimidate them. He did not fully succeed.
He talked about 'making *Capital* more accessible to the working
class, a consideration which to me outweighs everything else',[7] but
this *was* talk. *Capital* was not, is not and never will be widely
accessible. To make it so, he would have had to use another style.
As it is, its impressive erudition and abstract complexity are
challenging to the few, but daunting and alienating to the many.

Theory alone is powerless. But it 'becomes a material force as
soon as it has gripped the masses'.[8] It has to be based in reality, to
grip people, to seize the imagination, to inspire, inform
and empower.

Ideas can never lead beyond an old world order but only beyond the ideas of the old world order. Ideas *cannot carry out anything at all*. In order to carry out ideas men are needed who can exert practical force.[9]

Marx set out to expose ideological fallacies by means of critique. Thus, having announced a critique of jurisprudence and political science, his plan was to

publish the critique of law, ethics, politics, etc., in a series of distinct, independent pamphlets, and afterwards try in a special work to present them again as a connected whole showing the interrelationship of the separate parts, and lastly attempt a critique of the speculative elaboration of that material.[10]

This project was never completed. After finishing *The German Ideology* (1847), Marx seldom used the term 'ideology'. But he continued to write about the politics of ideas, showing how ideas are connected to power relations. For instance, he wrote about English antagonism towards the Irish.

This antagonism is kept artificially alive and intensified by the press, the pulpit, the comic papers, in short by all the means at the disposal of the ruling class. This antagonism is the secret of the English working class's impotence, despite its organisation. It is the secret of the maintenance of power by the capitalist class. And the latter is fully aware of this.[11]

Although the word 'ideology' does not appear, this passage is talking about the political power of the Church and the press – and the effects of popular culture.

Ideology is also about what is not said. For instance, during the Opium Wars against China, when the British were forcing imports of opium into China, as if to turn it into a colony, Marx accused the mainstream press of trying to 'divert investigation from the main issue'.

We hear nothing of the illicit opium trade, which yearly feeds the British treasury at the expense of human life and morality. We hear nothing of the constant bribery of sub-officials, by means of which the Chinese government is defrauded of its rightful revenue on incoming and outgoing merchandise .... We hear nothing of all this and of much more, first, because the majority of people out of China care little about the social and moral condition of that country; and secondly, because it is the part of policy and prudence not to agitate topics where no pecuniary advantage would result. Thus, the English people at home, who look no further than the grocer's where they buy their tea, are prepared to swallow all the misrepresentations which the Ministry and the Press choose to thrust down the public throat.[12]

After the Paris Commune, 'all the sluices of slander at the disposal of the venal, respectable press' and 'the lying power of the civilised world' were again in action to demonise the First International, in a 'war of calumny' waged by 'all shades of ruling class opinion'.[13]

Marx is constantly asking of received ideas

- what premises does this defend or conceal?
- what are its links with power, oppression and liberation?

His notion of ideology stems from his theory of history. He wants to show how the real world, especially the socioeconomic world, is the basis of our ideas and ideals. For example, actual commerce comes first; the law of contract second.

> First there is *commerce* and then a *legal system* develops out of it ... in developed bartering the participants tacitly acknowledge one another as equal persons and owners of the respective goods to be exchanged by them; they already *do* that while offering their goods to each other and agreeing to trade with each other. This *actual* relation, which only arises through and in the exchange, is later given the *legal form* in the contract, etc. ... .[14]

It is not just that commerce is a prerequisite for commercial law, although evidently it is. Marx makes the much wider claim that 'the exchange of exchange values is the real productive basis of all equality and freedom. As pure ideas, equality and freedom are merely idealised expressions of this exchange ...'.[15]

Other Meanings of 'Ideology'

Although the notion of 'ideology' is particularly associated with Marx, it is not his exclusively. The word was coined by a Frenchman, Destutt de Tracey, in the eighteenth century. He used it positively, to denote the rigorous study of ideas, the 'positive science of ideas'. The term was given its pejorative twist by Napoleon Bonaparte, who used it more to mean distorted thought. Now, ideology has a whole range of meanings and connotations, positive, neutral and negative:

- the study of ideas: how they are produced, packaged and passed on, how they are used and abused;
- beliefs or belief systems which run people's lives and influence how they act;
- how values and meanings are produced and passed on;

- the medium through which we interpret and make sense of our social world;
- forms of thought arising from our place in society,
- ideas, attitudes and illusions of a social group or class;
- ideas which serve the interests of a social group;
- false notions which legitimate a dominant group, or disempower an oppressed one;
- 'prolefeed': lies and distractions spread by the media;
- how inequality and oppression are made to seem natural.

Amongst the many writers influenced by Marx who have tried to show how thought is socially conditioned is the Russian philosopher, Mikhail Bakhtin.

> Individual consciousness is not the architect of the ideological superstructure, but only a tenant lodging in the social edifice of ideological signs.[16]

Karl Mannheim developed the 'sociology of knowledge', which elaborates many of Marx's ideas, whilst discarding notions of class struggle and proletarian revolution. The Italian Marxist Antonio Gramsci used the idea of 'hegemony' to explain how rulers govern, on the whole, by consent rather than force. The French philosopher Louis Althusser distinguished between the Repressive State Apparatus (RSA), meaning the army, police etc., and the Ideological State Apparatus (ISA), meaning the media, education, etc. The ISA conducts what Marx once called 'the whole manufacture of public opinion'.[17] Michel Foucault distrusts the word 'ideology', but explores similar areas, with a special focus on power. He looks not so much at what thought *is*, but more at what it *does*.

> Thought is no longer theoretical. As soon as it functions, it offends or reconciles, attracts or repels, breaks, dissociates, unites or reunites. It cannot help but liberate and enslave. Even before prescribing, suggesting a future, saying what must be done, even before exhorting or merely sounding an alarm, thought, at the level of its existence, in its very dawning, is in itself an action – a perilous act.[18]

Stuart Hall has noted how the 'manufacture of public opinion' especially involves the setting of a news agenda. Some issues are headlines; some are two lines on page 15; some are totally ignored. The stories chosen reinforce some views and undermine others. They can create and exploit anxieties, or deflect them into moral panics about youth subcultures. Issues are personalised, trivialised, sensationalised or ignored.

There's been nothing about ostriches in the papers for months; somebody's either building an ostrich monopoly or herding them into concentration camps.[19]

Questions

1. Is knowledge power?
2. What is the difference between knowledge and ideology? How can the two be fully separated?
3. Is it fair to say that academics are 'servants of the State'?
4. To what extent is education class-based and class-biased?
5. What do we mean by 'western' thought?
6. What evidence, if any, is there that 'cultural capital' (knowledge) is ethnocentric (biased to the interests of the dominant ethnic group), androcentric (man-centred) and middle class?
7. 'The ideas of the ruling class are in every epoch the ruling ideas.' Are they?
8. Are some kinds of knowledge (for example, abstract knowledge) better remunerated than others (for example, emotional skills)? If so, what does this tell us?

CHAPTER 10

Philosophy

> ... philosophers do not spring up like mushrooms out of the ground; they are products of their time, of their nation, whose most subtle, valuable and invisible juices flow in the ideas of philosophy. The same spirit that constructs railways with the hands of workers, constructs philosophical systems in the brains of philosophers.[1]

This chapter

- uses Marx's notion of ideology to introduce his philosophy;
- says what he was trying to do through philosophy;
- explains what he meant by 'materialism' and 'dialectics';
- sketches his relationship to Hegel;
- rejects attempts to reduce his philosophy to a single, unified method;
- instead, considers his writing as a mix of several elements: 'praxis', 'critique', 'serious study' and 'science';
- discusses what he meant by 'laws';
- argues that his work was not 'scientific', in the usual modern sense of the word;
- points out the diversity of his philosophical writings;
- summarises his ideas about liberty and human rights;
- suggests that he did have distinctive ideas about ontology; namely an emphasis that both the world and human experience are socially constructed;
- cites some stray remarks on language;
- notes the transdisciplinary character of his philosophy;
- illustrates the strengths and weaknesses of his approach by reference to one passage.

Philosophy as Ideology

What Marx wrote about ideology in general, he applied to philosophy in particular.

Philosophy and Society. Marx wanted to show how 'theoretical bubble-blowing' has 'its origin in actual earthly relations'.[2] The philosophical claim to be above or outside society is a pretence. Philosophy participates in the grubby reality of the age. (And reality, should a philosopher enquire, is what actually happens in

81

banks, houses, prisons, schools, offices, police stations, hospitals and barracks.)

Philosophy and Oppression. Marx thought that philosophy propagated and reinforced the ideas of the ruling class. This it could do intellectually (for example, by making 'passing historical phases' like private property appear natural and eternal); or practically, by churning out 'graduated flunkies' (as Lenin called them) to serve the state.

Philosophy and Liberation. But philosophy had the potential to be otherwise; it could explain, illuminate and inspire.

> The philosophers have only *interpreted* the world in various ways; the point, however, is to *change* it.[3]

Clearly a progressive philosophy could not be the kind which discussed how many angels can cavort on a pin. In place of 'drunken speculation', Marx called for 'sober philosophy', which recognises the material world as existing in its own right.

Materialism

Such a philosophy, in Marx's view, was materialism. This means acknowledging the primacy of the physical world, seeing it as the ultimate reality. By contrast, idealism takes the phenomena of the mind as the ultimate reality.[4]

The materialist outlook, for Marx, is closely linked to science and secularism. Copernicus made his 'great discoveries on the true solar system', by ignoring Church dogma. Various thinkers – Machiavelli, Hobbes, Spinoza, Rousseau, Fichte and Hegel – had begun to analyse the state 'from reason and experience, and not from theology'.[5] Marx admired the *philosophes* of the French Enlightenment: Voltaire, Condorcet, Mirabeau and Montesquieu. The main materialist influence on him from Germany was Ludwig Feuerbach, to whom we shall return.

For Marx, in the first instance, materialism stands for reason and science, against superstition and deception. He especially admired the scientific outlook of Francis Bacon, the 'real progenitor of *English materialism* and all *modern experimental* science'.

> According to him the *senses* are infallible and are the *source* of all knowledge. All science is based on *experience* and consists in subjecting the data furnished by the senses to a *rational method* of investigation. Induction, analysis, comparison, observation, experiment are the principal forms of such a rational method.[6]

Marx wanted a materialism which included the historical process and intangible but nonetheless real social relations; which started out from 'the actual given relations of life' and from that showed how this reality has been mystified or apotheosised.[7]

Hegel and Dialectics

As well as starting out from real life, a progressive philosophy should also acknowledge the importance of change. In this respect Marx looked to Hegel (1770–1831), the pre-eminent European philosopher of the time. Contradiction and change are key categories for Hegel. In this sense, his thought was 'dialectical'. Marx liked that. He wanted to alter, apply and revolutionise Hegel.

Hegel saw history as the development and self-realisation of the Mind (or *Geist* in German). *Geist* was the key to history, the motor of human development. For Marx this was just pie-in-the-sky idealism. Hegel would have to be transformed into something more down-to-earth, matter-of-fact, materialist.

In direct contrast to German philosophy which descends from heaven to earth, here it is a matter of ascending from earth to heaven ... setting out from real, active men and on the basis of their real life-process demonstrating the development of the ideological reflexes and echoes of this life-process.[8]

Hegel would have to be turned the right way up. Keep the dialectical side; keep seeing things in terms of contradiction and change. But start out from real life; make it materialist. That was Marx's approach. He kept many of Hegel's terms and categories, but gave them new contexts and new meanings, as he applied them to history and political economy.

Hegel is the search-light with which Marx probes the recesses of Adam Smith and David Ricardo, what they had written and what they had ignored. Marx uses Hegelian dichotomies, such as essence/appearance; concrete/abstract; particular/universal; synthesis/analysis. He lets one discourse, Hegelianism, react with another, political economy, with, to his mind, explosive results. To others, the results were turgid and baffling, for by the time *Capital* came out (1867), Hegel was no longer in intellectual vogue. Indeed, Marx could probably only have written the work because he had been in exile in London for nearly 20 years, insulated from the new intellectual fashions in Germany. For him, the insights of Hegel were ever fresh.

When Marx, as a student, first came to Hegel, the Hegelians had split two ways: some conservative, some radical. The original writings of Hegel are notoriously arcane and there were two distinct ways of simplifying him to a point of comprehension. For instance, he had written gnomically: 'whatever is real is rational'. His conservative followers could say that the reactionary Prussian state

was real and therefore had to be rational. The radical Young
Hegelians – amongst whom we may number Bruno Bauer, David
Friedrich Strauss, Arnold Ruge, Feuerbach and Marx – drew the
opposite conclusion. The Prussian state was irrational and therefore
impermanent.

Marx's early works are a dialogue with Hegel,[9] as well as a
diatribe against Young Hegelians. On completing *The German
Ideology* (1846), Marx felt that he had settled accounts with his
former philosophic consciousness and achieved his main purpose
– self-clarification.[10] In 1847, he gives a hostile, unfair summary
of Hegel in *The Poverty of Philosophy*.[11] With the upheavals of
1848, Hegel drops into the background. In 1853 Marx is describing
him as 'a most profound yet fantastic speculator'.[12] But in 1857
when Marx returns to his economic project, Hegel, with his ideas
about 'totality' and contradiction, stages a return. 'What was of
great use to me as regards *method* of treatment was Hegel's
Logic ...'.[13] Marx pays tribute to Hegel as the first to present the
dialectic 'in a comprehensive and conscious manner', adding that,
properly understood, the dialectic

> is a scandal and an abomination to the bourgeoisie and its
> doctrinaire spokesmen, because it includes in its positive
> understanding of what exists a simultaneous recognition of its
> negation, its inevitable destruction; because it regards every
> historically developed form as being in a fluid state, in motion,
> and therefore grasps its transient aspect as well; and because it
> does not let itself be impressed by anything, being in its very
> essence critical and revolutionary.[14]

Dialectics is a way of understanding things as stages in a process.
It seeks out 'contradictions', not in the sense of logical impos-
sibilities, but of inner stresses and opposing forces. These are then
used to explain the 'essence' of a thing – its intrinsic potentialities
for change.

Feuerbach

After Hegel, the second major philosopher to influence Marx was
Ludwig Feuerbach, whose *Essence of Christianity* (1841) argued that
God is an idea on to which we project our humanity. 'The
personality of God is nothing else than the projected personality
of man.'[15] Feuerbach was proposing that the material world comes
first and the conceptual world second. 'Being is the subject: thought
is the predicate.'

Marx's 'Theses on Feuerbach' were written in 1845, when he
was starting to see the inadequacy of Feuerbach's work. Engels
extracted them from Marx's notebook and published them in 1888

under their present title. Marx argues that we should see reality as
'sensuous human activity'. We should look at 'the active side' and
see 'human activity itself as objective activity'. He concludes with
his famous statement about changing the world.

> The philosophers have only interpreted the world in various
> ways; the point however is to change it.[16]

A Unified System?

According to orthodox Marxist-Leninists, Marx perfected his own
philosophy: dialectical materialism. His work was (i) about matter
and material realities and (ii) about change and fluidity, about
process. Others have sought to characterise Marx's method in
other terms. It has been called 'structural-genetic analysis';[17] and
'dialectical phenomenology', to indicate that it treats ideas and
individuals as grounded in a historically specific form of life, which
is a totality of internal relations and which, being contradictory, is
set to change.[18]

Alternatively we could see Marx's philosophy as a mix of several
elements:

1. 'praxis': using ideas to change the world;
2. 'critique': helping people to see through appearances and
   illusions and to understand essence (*Capital* is subtitled *A
   Critique of Political Economy*);
3. 'dialectics': applying the method of Hegelian dialectics in a
   materialist context;
4. 'serious study': considered enquiry into things, which is based
   on analysis of evidence more than prejudice; 'social science';
5. 'science' in a stricter sense; positivism; the claim that he is
   discovering laws; that his work is like natural science and
   deserves the same status in respect of the truths it uncovers.

There are tensions between these different kinds of writing, with
the differing claims each makes about the kind of knowledge it is
offering and the degree to which it is being 'scientific'.

Science, Laws and Positivism

Marx talks about 'laws', but he uses the word as political economists
did at the time, more loosely than we now would. He was *not* talking
about laws in the sense of uniform and universally valid
relationships of cause and effect, where one event regularly follows
another. Thus, when he writes of the 'natural laws of capitalist
production', he quietly concedes that these 'laws' might really be
just 'tendencies'. 'It is a question of these laws, of these tendencies,

winning their way through and working themselves out with iron necessity.'[19] After describing some features of capitalism, he summarises:

> *This is the absolute general law of capitalist accumulation.* Like all other laws, it is modified in its working by many circumstances, the analysis of which does not concern us here.[20]

This proposes an absolute law; then admits that it needs modifying; but skips over the details. The procedure divides phenomena into (a) significant laws and (b) countervailing tendencies. It ignores the possibility that the second category might be as significant as the first; and indeed might have an equal claim to be called 'laws'.

Social 'laws', according to Marx, are not eternal, but valid only within a particular historical context.

> ... every particular historical mode of production has its own special laws of population, which are historically valid within that particular sphere.[21]

Of course, Marx is himself using the word 'law' within a particular historical context, where, for instance (bourgeois) political economists spoke about the 'laws' of supply and demand and other supposed economic laws, often used to keep the working class in its place. Marx denounces the ahistorical 'laws' of orthodox economics and to some extent his 'laws' are in response to their 'laws'. The word 'law' becomes ammunition in the battle. It has a rhetorical function: to respond to others in their own terms, to suggest a commitment to rigour, to convey some of the ambition, excitement and potential of his plan, as when he declares that 'it is the ultimate aim of this work [*Capital*] to reveal the economic laws of motion of modern society'.[22]

Whatever he himself thought, Marx's work is not scientific in the positivist sense.[23] He did not specify methods of verification or falsification for his predictions. And he certainly did not investigate cause–effect relationships through repeatable double trials, in which subjects are randomly assigned to two groups and in which all factors are kept the same except one variable. Given the time that he was living and the nature of what he was writing about, that was impossible. Nor is Marx's work scientific in an important, looser sense. For whereas the true scientist seeks out what would *disprove* a hypothesis, Marx neglects awkward evidence in his overriding mission to *corroborate* preconceptions. In *Capital*, for instance, his priority is to expose dreadful working conditions, so he makes light of the Factory Acts, which were beginning to alleviate the worst excesses. He underestimates the extent to which capitalism could regulate itself.

Rather than reducing Marx's work to a single approach – or set of approaches – it is more fruitful to consider instead the breadth and variety of his writings. He had the knack of getting to the heart of a subject, sometimes just in an analogy or aside. He made a trenchant contribution to the philosophy of religion. Through socialist realism and critical theory, he had a significant (and often stultifying) impact on aesthetics. He also had far-reaching ideas about political and moral philosophy.

Political Philosophy

Marx criticises conventional ('liberal') human rights for being too abstract, too limited. What it calls liberty is just 'the liberty of man as an isolated monad, withdrawn into himself'.[24] If liberty is conceptualised in this narrow way, then 'the practical application of man's right to liberty is man's right to private property'. This in turn boils down to 'the right to enjoy one's property and to dispose of it at one's discretion, without regard to other men, independently of society, the right of self-interest'. And this 'makes every man see in other men not the realisation of his own freedom, but the barrier to it'.

> None of the so-called rights of man, therefore, go beyond egoistic man, beyond man as a member of civil society, that is, an individual withdrawn into himself, into the confines of his private interests and private caprice, and separated from the community.[25]

Society then 'appears as a framework external to the individuals, as a restriction of their original independence'. The sole bond holding people together is 'natural necessity, need and private interest, the preservation of their property and their egoistic selves'.

Instead of all this, Marx calls for a larger and more positive understanding of liberty, based on 'the association of man with man'. It should recognise man as a 'species-being', living a 'species-life' in community. And this new understanding should go hand in hand with a revolution in society.

> Only when the real, individual man re-absorbs in himself the abstract citizen, and as an individual human being has become a *species-being* in his everyday life, in his particular work, and in his particular situation, only when man has recognised and organised his *'forces propres'* [own powers] as *social* forces, and consequently no longer separates social power from himself in the shape of *political* power, only then will human emancipation have been accomplished.[26]

The Social Construction of Reality

Marx has his own ideas about the nature of reality. At times he takes a straightforward materialist position: 'the ideal is nothing but the material world reflected in the mind of man, and translated into forms of thought'.[27] This position is developed and defended by Lenin, especially in *Materialism and Empiriocriticism*; and became the orthodoxy in Soviet Marxism.

But Marx also has a more interesting position, emphasised in more humanist currents of Marxism, which stresses 'praxis'. He insists that the 'sensuous world' is 'not a thing given direct from all eternity, remaining ever the same, but the product of industry and of the state of society'.[28] Our experience is 'an historical product, the result of the activity of a whole succession of generations'. Take a cherry-tree for example.

> The cherry-tree, like almost all fruit-trees, was, as is well known, only a few centuries ago transplanted by *commerce* into our zone, and therefore only *by* this action of a definite society in a definite age has it become 'sensuous certainty'... .[29]

The same goes for human nature. We are not trans-historical or metaphysical beings. 'The individual *is the social being*'[30] and 'just as society itself produces man as man, so is society produced by him'.[31] It follows that 'the history of a single individual cannot possibly be separated from the history of preceding or contemporary individuals, but is determined by this history'.[32]

Humans are not just material in the sense of flesh and blood, or chemical compounds and molecules. We have an intrinsic social dimension to our existence.

> ... a man first sees and recognises himself in another man. Peter only relates to himself as a man through his relation to another man, Paul, in whom he recognises his likeness.[33]

Language

Part of being social is language and some of Marx's stray remarks anticipate the twentieth-century concern with language and linguistics.

> Language is as old as consciousness, language *is* practical, real consciousness that exists for other men as well, and only therefore does it also exist for me ... . Consciousness is, therefore, from the very beginning a social product, and remains so as long as men exist at all.[34]

On another occasion Marx elides 'the material intercourse of man' with 'the language of real life', by putting the one in apposition to the other.

> The production of ideas, of conceptions, of consciousness is at first directly interwoven with the material activity and the material intercourse of men, the language of real life.[35]

Praxis

In his 'Theses on Feuerbach', Marx attacks the 'ivory tower' mentality and urges a link between theory and practice (praxis). He equates truth (*Wahrheit*) with reality (*Wirklichkeit*), power (*Macht*) and 'this-sidedness' (*Diesseitigkeit*). This suggests that the truth does not reside in some pure or autonomous realm of philosophy, but is something to be realised through its power to manifest in reality.

In Marx's view, perception and sensation are not merely a reflection of the world. Rather, they are the result of an interaction (a dialectic) between 'sensuous human activity' and our surroundings. *We actively process and construct our experience.*

> For instance, one man is king only because other men stand in the relation of subjects to him. They, on the other hand, imagine that they are subject because he is king.[36]

Human character is socially constructed and for this very reason we have the potential to be otherwise.

> To be a slave, to be a CITIZEN are social determinations, relations between human beings A and B. Human being A, as such, is not a slave; he is a slave in and through society.[37]

Marx argues that our desires and pleasures spring from society and are relative to society.[38] He sees 'reality' itself as 'human sensuous activity, practice'.

> All social life is essentially *practical*. All mysteries which lead theory to mysticism find their rational solution in human practice and in the comprehension of this practice.[39]

This notion of practice implies a complex interplay of mind, culture, society and activity. Something of this interplay is evident in Marx's philosophy of history, which allows for both a structural approach (how structures operate) and a more 'interpretative' outlook, which puts the focus on how people interact with their world to create 'reality'. He starts out from practical matters: how people organise to meet their needs, 'eating and drinking, housing, clothing and various other things'. These practical needs 'must daily and hourly be fulfilled in order to sustain human life'.[40] In returning to 'the real process of production' and 'the real ground of history', Marx thinks he has exposed 'the actual social relations which give rise to' the 'idealistic humbug' of philosophy.[41]

All this depends on a particular notion of reality and what is most 'real'. For Marx, reality is, in the first place,

> a sum of productive forces, a historically created relation to nature and of individuals to one another, which is handed down to each generation from its predecessor; a mass of productive forces, capital funds and circumstances, which on the one hand is indeed modified by the new generation, but on the other also prescribes for it its conditions of life and gives it a definite development, a special character.[42]

Reality and Interdisciplinarity

If philosophy is the study of reality, it must quit the ivory tower and sally forth to study technology, society, economics and history. Marx thought that he had done this. For instance he wrote about technology – how it has developed, its social impact and its relation to human needs. If philosophy is locked into social reality, then it ceases to exist as an independent branch of knowledge. Marx therefore announced the death of (pure) philosophy.

> Where speculation ends, where real life starts, there consequently begins real, positive science, the expounding of the practical activity, of the practical process of development of men. Empty phrases about consciousness end, and real knowledge has to take their place. When the reality is described, philosophy as an independent branch of knowledge [die selbständige Philosophie] loses its medium of existence.[43]

He compares philosophy with masturbation.

> One has to 'leave philosophy aside' ... one has to leap out of it and devote oneself like an ordinary man to the study of actuality, for which there exists also an enormous amount of material, unknown, of course, to the philosophers ... . Philosophy and the study of the actual world have the same relation to one another as onanism and sexual love.[44]

Instead of the 'one-sided, crippled development' of thought, Marx calls for thinking which has more 'universality', springing from a 'many-sided life' which 'embraces a wide circle of varied activities and practical relations to the world'. This kind of thought is 'always a factor in the total life of the individual'.

In the case of an individual, for example, whose life embraces a wide circle of varied activities and practical relations to the world, and who, therefore, lives a many-sided life, thought has the same character of universality as every other manifestation of his life. Consequently, it neither becomes fixed in the form of abstract thought nor does it need complicated tricks of reflection when the individual passes from thought to some other manifestation of life. From the outset it is always a factor in the total life of the individual, one which disappears and is reproduced as *required*.[45]

An Example

Marx tests and transgresses the conventions of pure philosophy by crossing in and out of the philosophical realms and jurisdiction. In mixing philosophy with political economy, history, sociology, politics, etc., the boundaries of each academic discipline are unravelled, or exposed as artificial and arbitrary.

To see some of the strengths and weaknesses of his approach – and something of its peculiarity – consider the passage below, from an early work, 'On the Jewish Question'.

> Let us consider the actual, worldly Jew, not the *Sabbath Jew*, as Bauer does, but the *everyday Jew*.
>
> Let us not look for the secret of the Jew in his religion, but let us look for the secret of his religion in the real Jew.
>
> What is the secular basis of Judaism? *Practical* need, *self-interest*.
>
> What is the worldly religion of the Jew? *Huckstering*. What is his worldly God? *Money*.
>
> Very well then! Emancipation from *huckstering* and *money*, consequently from practical, real Judaism, would be the self-emancipation of our time.[46]

Marx proposes to start out from 'the actual, worldly Jew'; and from this to find the 'secret of religion'. He proceeds to argue with enormous and unwarranted confidence, punning on the words 'Jude' and 'Judentum', which refer to both 'Jewishness' and usury, commerce, trading, or as Marx disparagingly calls it, 'huckstering'. To some extent he is using simple prejudice. He produces no evidence that self-interest is 'the secular basis of Judaism'. He merely states it as if it were self-evident; and ignores whether self-interest is equally the secular basis of other belief systems. Rather than discussing anti-Semitism and its causes, he dramatically broadens or twists the argument to call for the abolition of the whole world of money.

The style is incisive and flamboyant; and the tone is polemical, attacking the position of Bruno Bauer. The critique is praxis in that it is part of a political project: to turn a contemporary debate about Judaism towards a debate about capitalism; to turn a religious question into a political one; and to offer a new meaning for 'emancipation'.

Questions

1. To what extent is philosophy a product and prisoner of its culture?
2. 'The purpose of philosophy is to explain, to fortify and to propagate the half truths manufactured by the bourgeoisie and so useful in consolidating its power.' (Paul Nizan, *Les Chiens de Garde.*) Is it?
3. 'Sober philosophy' or 'drunken speculation': which predominates in Marx's work?
4. What is 'materialism'?

CHAPTER 11

Exploitation and Economics

This chapter provides a sympathetic account of Marx's economics and then indicates the problems it raises.

Marx's Intentions

One way to make sense of Marx's writing is to start out from his likely intentions. Marx is trying to

- analyse why society is as it is;
- show how inequalities are reproduced, day to day;
- explain the exploitation he saw around him;
- have that exploitation not just denounced, but *proved* and *quantified;*
- move from indignation and outrage to analysis and understanding;
- demolish contemporary ('bourgeois') political economy, with its implicit and explicit support of exploitation;
- expose capitalism as unstable and prone to crisis;
- write economics for working people.

Marx wanted to explain how societies work and thus to make socialism more 'scientific'. For him, political economy was not just an abstract, academic subject. It examined real things: work, wages, money, class, the impact of new technology, etc. He aimed to 'reveal the economic law of motion of modern society';[1] and to enquire into the power of the capitalist, the limits of that power and the character of those limits.[2] 'Economics is not concerned with things but with relations between persons, and in the final analysis between classes; these relations, however, are always *bound to things* and *appear as things*.'[3]

Marx criticised existing political economy for ignoring historical factors to do with class, power and oppression. Instead of *explaining* why the rich are rich and the poor are poor, it just took class division as a given. This was wrong, analytically and morally.

> Political economy starts with the fact of private property; it does not explain it to us .... Political economy throws no light on the cause of the division between labour and capital, and between capital and land. When, for example, it defines the relationship

of wages to profit, it takes the interest of the capitalists to be
the ultimate cause, i.e., it takes for granted what it is supposed
to explain ... . The only wheels which political economy sets in
motion are *greed* and the *war amongst the greedy – competition*.[4]

Marx's disagreement with political economy was absolutely
fundamental. He was criticising the entire perspective which, he
said, took too much for granted. It failed to explain key issues, such
as property, inequality and exploitation. Its categories were not
'worthy of our human nature'.[5]

Marx set out to put this straight. His first main critique of
political economy is the *Economic and Philosophic Manuscripts* of
1844. This focuses on the alienating effect of money, the exchange
economy and capitalism. Marx explained his basic ideas in two
short works, now known as *Wage Labour and Capital* and *Value,
Price and Profit*. His more detailed manuscripts of 1857–58 are now
published as the *Grundrisse*. In 1859 he published his *Contribution
to the Critique of Political Economy*. Between 1861 and 1863, he wrote
a huge economic manuscript, from which Engels later edited the
second and third volumes of *Capital* and Kautsky extracted *Theories
of Surplus Value*. The first volume of *Capital* was published in
1867.

Marx thought that the 'discoveries' outlined in these works were
his main achievement. This is how he described his vast project in
a letter of 1858.

> The whole thing is to be divided into six books: 1. On Capital.
> 2. Landed Property. 3. Wage Labour. 4. State. 5. International
> Trade. 6. World Market.[6]

Although he completed only the first volume on capital, Marx
believed that he had done enough to set political economy on a
whole new basis.

Exploitation

What makes Marx's work relevant is his focus on exploitation. By
way of example, consider the cost of a sports shoe (see Table
11.1).

The shoe sells for $70, but only $1.66 goes to labour. Labour –
mostly young women in Thailand – is 2.3 per cent of the retail
price.[7] A good example of exploitation.

In his quest to expose and define exploitation, Marx constantly
asks two simple questions: Who works? and Who profits?

This takes us back to the basic history of property and
expropriation. Peasants had been driven from their land and their

livelihood through a long historical process, in England called 'enclosure'.[8] These ex-peasants, evicted from the land, now had to find work with someone (a capitalist). They became workers (proletarians). In Marx's terms, they are obliged to sell their labour power. Their work is what produces wealth for the capitalist. To use a Marxist cliche it is 'the goose that lays the golden egg'. 'Property is the fruit of labour ... of others.'[9]

Table 11.1: The cost of a sports shoe

The Nike Air Pegasus Shoe	
Materials	$9.18
Labour	$1.66
Subcontractor's profit	$1.19
Admin and overheads	$2.82
= Total ex-factory price	$14.85
Plus transport, costs and profit	$22.95
= Total wholesale price	$37.80
Retail price	$70.00

Whatever the society, someone always has to work, if only to provide food and shelter. The amount of time spent on producing the means to survive – the means of subsistence – Marx calls 'necessary labour'. It is necessary for both the worker in general and the capitalist world in particular, 'because the continued existence of the worker is the basis of that world'.[10] Workers, however, generally do more than is necessary just to subsist. On top of the 'necessary labour' they also perform 'surplus labour'. This is what 'creates surplus-value which, for the capitalist, has all the charms of something created out of nothing'.[11]

Under feudalism the distinction between 'necessary' and 'surplus' labour is glaringly obvious. The time peasants spend on their own patch is 'necessary labour'; and the days toiling on the baron's estate are 'surplus labour'. Under capitalism the distinction is not so apparent. When workers get their wage packet or salary, it is not clear how much corresponds to 'necessary' labour and how much is 'surplus' labour. But, according to Marx, even if the distinction is invisible, it is still important.

Capitalists buy the ability to do work ('labour power') in exchange for wages. In other words, labour power is a commodity. But it is a unique commodity, because unlike any other, it *produces value*. More to the point, it also produces surplus value.

Capital ... is essentially the command over unpaid labour. All surplus-value, whatever particular form (profit, interest or rent)

it may subsequently crystallise into, is in substance the materi-
alisation of unpaid labour-time.[12]

Capitalists get workers to turn raw materials into commodities
which can then be sold at a profit. They buy labour power for less
than it produces. It creates value for them. Money doesn't create
wealth; workers create wealth. On the subject of surplus value, Marx
was adamant: 'there is not one single atom of its value that does
not own its existence to unpaid labour'. Even if capitalists give
decent wages, 'the whole thing still remains the age-old activity of
the conqueror, who buys commodities from the conquered with
the money he has stolen from them'.[13]

There was at the time a debate about the nature of exploitation.
Proudhon, the French socialist, argued that exploitation came
from unequal exchange – and the remedy was to establish co-ops
and state banks. Marx disagreed. In a few special instances profit
may come from selling commodities above their value, by
surcharging or trickery in exchange. But that is not the general,
systematic source of profit. For what one dealer gains, another must
lose. 'The capitalist class of a given country, taken as a whole,
cannot defraud itself.'[14] Marx insisted that exploitation ultimately
has to do with how capitalists control labour power.

Capital ... pumps out a certain specific quantum of surplus
labour from the direct producers or workers, surplus labour that
it receives without an equivalent and which by its very nature
always remains forced labour, however much it might appear
as the result of free contractual agreement. This surplus labour
is expressed in a surplus-value, and this surplus-value exists in
a surplus product ... .[15]

To explain the general nature of profits, Marx assumes that 'on an
average, commodities are sold at their real value, and that profits
are derived from selling them at their values, that is, in proportion
to the quantity of labour realised in them'.[16] Exploitation arises
from production, not from exchange.

Capitalists want to increase surplus labour, to increase profit. In
Marx's time, the most obvious way to do this was just to lengthen
the working day. Workers in Europe then worked as long as many
now do in the 'Third World'. Some had a 16-hour day. In England,
the Factory Acts of 1850 had limited work to 12 hours a day
during the week and 8 hours on Saturday. Allowing for breaks, this
meant 60 working hours a week. The fight to enforce and reinforce
the Factory Acts was one of the main political struggles of
the time.[17]

Another way to increase surplus value is to force wages down.
In the absence of a welfare state and strong unions, this could be

done by having a mass of people so desperate for work that they would be willing to labour for almost nothing. This 'reserve army of labour', as Marx calls it, would undercut the wages of those in work. Note that Marx is interested in 'the power of capital over labour'. This is the power to have Thai women labouring for a pittance; and the power to make 'flexible labour markets' and job insecurity.

Up to a point, Marx's emphasis on the role of labour was quite orthodox for the time. Think of the opening lines of Adam Smith's *Wealth of Nations*: 'The annual labour of every nation is the fund which originally supplies it with all the necessaries and conveniences of life ...'. Smith and David Ricardo had believed that the value of something ultimately derives from labour that has gone into making it. This idea – the 'labour theory of value' – was taken over by Marx, who then drew revolutionary conclusions about exploitation and the source of 'surplus value'. But his (uncritical) acceptance of the labour theory of value is also the chief flaw in his theory of exploitation.

Problems: the Labour Theory of Value

To understand the labour theory of value, we must first distinguish between 'use value' and 'exchange value'. The use value is the usefulness of an object. The 'exchange value' is the value it exchanges for. Economics is mainly about exchange values. If you buy a car, what matters economically is what you pay and how much you sell it on for. The usefulness of the car – its use value – matters to you, but not to the economist. Use value and exchange value are not necessarily related. Air, for example, has a great use value, but zero exchange value.

According to the labour theory of value, the exchange value of any commodity (for example, the car) depends on the amount of 'social labour' which has gone into it. See how Marx puts it.

> A commodity has *a value*, because it is a *crystallisation of social labour*. The *greatness* of its value, or its *relative* value, depends upon the greater or less amount of that social substance contained in it; that is to say, on the relative mass of labour necessary for its production.[18]

Marx anticipates and counters some of the obvious objections to this.

> It might seem that if the value of a commodity is determined by the *quantity of labour bestowed upon its production,* the lazier a man, or the clumsier a man, the more valuable his commodity, because the greater the time of labour required for finishing the

commodity. This, however, would be a sad mistake. You will recollect that I used the word *'Social* labour', and many points are involved in this qualification of *'Social'*. In saying that the value of a commodity is determined by the *quantity of labour* worked up or crystallised in it, we mean *the quantity of labour necessary* for its production in a given state of society, under certain social average conditions of production, with a given social average intensity, and average skill of the labour employed.[19]

In other words, 'social' or 'abstract' labour depends on various factors, including the state of technology at the time. (Technology can be seen as the product of past labour.) The point is illustrated with an example.

When, in England, the power-loom came to compete with the hand-loom, only one half of the former time of labour was wanted to convert a given amount of yarn into a yard of cotton or cloth. The poor hand-loom weaver now worked seventeen or eighteen hours daily, instead of the nine or ten hours he had worked before. Still the product of twenty hours of his labour represented now only ten social hours of labour, or ten hours of labour socially necessary for the conversion of a certain amount of yarn into textile stuffs. His product of twenty hours had, therefore, no more value than his former product of ten hours.[20]

Trying to calculate that value becomes a very complex business indeed. We have to take into account not just the amount of social labour going into the product, but also the amount that went into the raw materials, machinery, etc. We have to calculate 'the quantity of labour *previously* worked up in the raw material of the commodity, and the labour bestowed on the implements, tools, machinery, and buildings, with which such labour is assisted'. Marx then gives an example of how complex the calculation of value would become.

For example, the value of a certain amount of cotton-yarn is the crystallisation of the quantity of labour added to the cotton during the spinning process, the quantity of labour previously realised in the cotton itself, the quantity of labour realised in the coal, oil and other auxiliary substances used, the quantity of labour fixed in the steam engine, the spindles, the factory building, and so forth ... as a spindle, for example, is but gradually used up, an average calculation is made, based upon the average time it lasts, and its average waste or wear and tear during a certain period, say a day. In this way we calculate how much of the value of the spindle is transferred to the yarn daily spun, and how much, therefore, of the total amount of labour realised in a pound of yarn, for example, is due to the quantity of labour previously realised in the spindle. For our present purpose it is not necessary to dwell any longer upon this point.[21]

Perhaps Marx does not 'dwell any longer upon this point' because to do so would get him entangled in Byzantine calculations of impossible complexity. For the 'quantity of labour' in each of the factors of production is not known with any certainty, so from the outset we are dealing with estimates and guesses and 'average calculations'. On top of this difficulty, we have to consider things like scenic coast-lines and rare jewels which could command a hefty price, even though no human work may have gone into them.

One way to cut through the Gordian knot would be to ditch the labour theory of value altogether and look instead at prices in terms of supply and demand. That is exactly what modern economics has done. For Marx, however, this is unsatisfactory because supply and demand explain only 'the temporary *fluctuations* of market prices'.

> You would be altogether mistaken in fancying that the value of labour or any other commodity whatever is ultimately fixed by supply and demand. Supply and demand regulate nothing but the temporary *fluctuations* of market prices. They will explain to you why the market price of a commodity rises above or sinks below its *value*, but they can never account for that *value* itself ... .[22]

A commodity has a value (based on the amount of social labour needed to make it). The actual price oscillates around that value, due to fluctuations in supply and demand. This creates something of a problem, which Marx acknowledges when he asks: 'What then is the relation between value and market prices, or between natural prices and market prices?'[23] Subsequent economists have delved deep into this can of worms, and all the detailed logical and theoretical problems seething inside it. They are collectively called the 'transformation problem'.

Another fundamental problem with Marx's approach concerns the meaning of 'social labour'. What is it we are averaging? The global average; the national average; the average within that sector? To take the example of the Nike sports shoe, how do you measure the work of the Thai women on the production line against the work involved in preparing marketing hype about 'tubular technology'?

Marx admits the problem. He asks: 'Is your hour's labour worth mine?' And he answers: 'That is a question which is decided by competition.'[24] That answer is true to an extent, perhaps self-evidently true. But it does not tell us how the Thai workers are being exploited – unless we say that the exploitation lies in the structure of competition, that is, in wider power relations. Marx follows Adam Smith in distinguishing truly productive labour from 'unproductive labour' – and sometimes he throws all the middle men into this second category, dismissing them as 'parasites' who 'interpose themselves between the capitalist and the wage-labourer'.[25] This kind of implicit abuse, even if it is justified, does not solve the problem. Heterogeneous work, going into the same product, cannot simply be boiled down into a homogenous mass of 'social labour'.

The concept of 'value' was fundamental in classical economics – the tradition in which Marx wrote. He accepted it as a 'scientific discovery'[26] and used it to come up with a theory of exploitation, which he believed was also 'scientific'. Modern economics has abandoned the notion. This was not just because 'bourgeois' economists were appalled when Marx used the concept to 'prove' exploitation – although doubtless many were. It was because other concepts better described actual, empirical change. Modern economics is more about supply, demand and price mechanisms. It studies efficiency rather than exploitation. It focuses on practical problems about economic decision-making. It eschews the concepts of value and surplus value. Marx's terminology is peripheral.

This change was already under way by the end of Marx's life. In the 1870s, Jevons, Walras and Menger (in England, Switzerland and Austria, respectively) were laying the foundations of modern ('neo-classical') economics. Unaware of their work, Marx never realised that they were the future of mainstream economics, not him. The marginalists would marginalise him.

Marx's theory of surplus value, ingenious and elaborate though it is, rests on shaky premises: the notion of 'value' (as distinct from price), the labour theory of value and the concept of 'abstract general labour'. These ideas are used with a kind of circular logic and do not fully explain actual economic changes. It is not just that the labour theory of value is wrong. The whole notion of value as a fundamental unit of analysis is mistaken.[27] 'Value' was an accepted convention at that time, but Marx mistakenly accepted it as an absolute truth.

The purpose of Marx's years in the British Museum Library was to uncover a 'law of surplus value', such that exploitation could be isolated, measured, proved, like a chemical substance. There is, however, no inherent reason why 'exploitation' should be able to be mapped on a single scale and quantified, any more than, say, love can be. But, like love, it is nonetheless real for that. It is a realm for the operation of human sympathy, as much as analytic prowess. We learn about it through imagination, compassion and fellow understanding.

In an important sense, people *know* in an immediate, practical way when exploitation is happening. It does not then need to be 'proved' in an abstract way. Indeed the abstraction may complicate and confuse what would otherwise be a straightforward, direct and felt realisation that exploitation is occurring. The danger is that in trying to make the concept of exploitation more precise, you end up making it more convoluted.

Although Marx's theory neglects the moral and emotional dimension of exploitation, his writing (for example, *Capital*) does include social and historical material and vivid descriptions of over-work and poverty. These convey something of the experience, facts and culture of exploitation, which cannot be expressed in pure mathematics or economics. Arguably they tell us more about exploitation than the theoretical sections on surplus value.[28] Likewise, in the case of the Thai women producing brand-name shoes, a breakdown of costs is instructive but the exploitation of these workers also involves their

- work conditions (long hours, few breaks, low pay [16 pence an hour], compulsory overtime);
- work experience (the drumming of machinery, the stink of glue, dangers of being dismembered);
- living conditions (four to a room, no electricity or running water, sewage in the streets);
- lack of power (a ban on free unions, fear of supervisors, job insecurity, lack of alternative choices).[29]

Marx knew that exploitation has to do with issues of power and unequal bargaining strengths. His efforts to explain it purely in terms of deductions from the labour theory of value were, though intellectually heroic, ultimately misguided.

Some Marxists have defended the labour theory of value despite its weaknesses. Others have sought a more plausible theory of exploitation. Chief among these is John Roemer. He analyses the grim logic of exploitation, which stems from unequal property relations and is reinforced by the labour market. Everyone is theoretically free to choose, but in practice choices are limited by birth and class. Only the already rich are economically free. The market is rigged by unequal property endowments. It is not a 'level playing field', so, as the 'game' proceeds, the disadvantaged are likely to lose more and more heavily. Put crudely, the rich get richer and the poor get poorer. Here is a *résumé* of his book.

Roemer sets out to solve the mystery of how there can be exploitation in a system without anyone being forced to work. Using (mathematical) game theory and assuming that people try to make rational choices about their own best interests, he shows how – in models where agents are endowed with unequal assets – the consequence of each following his or her own self-interest will be that some hire others to work for them and others must sell their labour in order to live. Class and exploitation emerge from free choice in a system where assets are unequally distributed.[30]

Roemer employs the neo-classical assumption that individuals make rational choices for optimisation under given constraints. In this way, he reconstructs the theory of exploitation in terms of rational choice. His basic unit of analysis is the individual agent: 'methodological individualism'. This contrasts with Marx's approach which was to emphasise the social rather than the individual. 'Society does not consist of individuals, but expresses the sum of the relationships and conditions in which these individuals stand to one another.'[31] But both would probably agree that we are socialised into choices and identities and then act more or less rationally to maximise our preferences.

So far I have been concentrating on the labour theory of value and Marx's account of exploitation because that is so central to his project. But his writings on political economy do not all fit under the rubric of exploitation; and it is time now to back up and consider some other aspects.

Marx's Approach

The obvious way to analyse a given country is to start with concrete facts: the population, classes, town and country, export and import, the nation, the state, etc. This is how the early political economists had proceeded in the seventeenth century. But, according to Marx, they had been mistaken. 'The correct scientific method' is to start out from 'a few determining abstract general relations', such as labour, division of labour, need, exchange value, and then advance to 'the State, international exchange and world market'. This approach 'leads from abstract determinations by way of thinking to the reproduction of the concrete'.[32]

To introduce Marx's economic ideas, I started out from 'labour' and the key role of work. But he began at a different place, with the commodity.[33] A commodity is anything that is bought and sold. *Capital* starts with an analysis of commodities in the abstract.

The wealth of societies in which the capitalist mode of production prevails appears as an 'immense collection of commodities';[34] the individual commodity appears as its elementary form. Our investigation therefore begins with the analysis of the commodity.[35]

This investigation leads into deep waters ...

> A commodity appears at first sight an extremely obvious, trivial thing. But its analysis brings out that it is a very strange thing, abounding in metaphysical subtleties and theological niceties.[36]

These 'subtleties' arise from the fact that the commodity is produced by human labour, and its value depends on human labour. But, by misunderstanding this, we fall prey to ...

Commodity Fetishism

A fetish is an object to which we attribute supernatural power, or on which we lavish undue attention. An example would be the old bones sold at inflated prices in Medieval Europe, because they were supposedly relics of saints. They were alleged to have miraculous properties in and of themselves (not because of what they symbolised). The old bone was fetishised. The Protestant Reformation abolished much of this religious superstition, but the new fetish, Marx thought, was what we sell our souls for: commodities.

That explains what might commonly be meant by 'commodity fetishism'. But Marx's own explanation is, typically, slightly different. He picks up the word from Hegel and Feuerbach and gives it a new twist. In his sense, 'fetishism' refers to how we see the economic values of things and how we ignore the labour theory of value and its ramifications. We usually think that the exchange value of something is due to the thing itself; as if its value were intrinsic to it, as if it were born with that value in its genes. According to Marx – and the labour theory of value – this is an illusion. 'So far', he wrote, 'no chemist has ever discovered exchange-value either in a pearl or a diamond.'[37] The value of something, according to Marx, is actually a social phenomenon which reflects the amount of social labour represented in it. This amount of labour is socially determined by existing conditions, the state of technology, etc. Fetishism, then, strictly, is the mistaken belief that the value of a commodity is intrinsic to it.[38] This generates fetishism in a looser sense, referring to the power of capitalist products.

> The rule of the capitalist over the worker is therefore the rule of the object over the human, of dead labour over living, of the product over the producer ... .[39]

This could be extended to social products, institutions and ideas, whose powers are not intrinsic properties, but human creations. 'Just as man is governed, in religion, by the products of his own brain, so, in capitalist production, he is governed by the products

of his own hand.'[40] He is also governed by the economic 'laws' of
capitalism and its tendency to stumble into crisis.

Crises

We saw earlier that surplus value can be increased by lengthening
the working day or cutting wages. But when workers are organised
both these options have high costs. A better way to extract more
surplus value is to increase the intensity of work through
mechanisation and improved technology. Marx believed, however,
that in the longer run this would lead to a 'tendency of the rate of
profit to fall'. To follow his reasoning here, we have to understand
a distinction between

(a) 'constant capital' – expenditure on raw materials, machinery,
    etc., and
(b) 'variable capital', which is wages.

Mechanisation leads to an increase in 'constant capital', both in
absolute terms and relative to 'variable capital' (wages). Marx calls
this the 'rising organic composition of capital'. But value, according
to the labour theory of value, springs from labour, or the part
represented by variable capital, which is diminishing. Marx thought
that this led to a tendency for the rate of profit to fall. This tendency
could, however, be 'held up, delayed and weakened by counter-
acting factors'.[41]

Marx believed that disproportions between the output of some
sectors led to economic crises.[42] Monetary reaction to these
disproportions could temporarily reduce aggregate demand below
aggregate supply. He expected crises to widen in scope as capitalism
itself spread. Generally, he understood the periodic business cycles
(expansion and recession), in terms of *over-production* and saw
them as an integral, irremediable feature of capitalism. Keynes later
reinterpreted it as a problem of *under-consumption*, which suggested
that the solution was state investment to prime pump the economy
and maintain demand.

Marx uses his critique of political economy to indicate what he
thinks the working class should do. He believes that the workers
will get poorer, perhaps in absolute terms, certainly relative to the
capitalists. (This is known as 'the immiseration of the proletariat'.)
The passage below suggests that workers should opt for revolution
even if they are getting richer.

> Wages are, above all, also determined by their relation to the
> gain, to the profit of the capitalist – comparative, relative
> wages ... . If, for instance, in times when business is good,

wages rise by 5%, profit on the other hand by 30%, then the comparative, the relative wages, have not *increased* but *decreased*.

Thus if the income of the worker increases with the rapid growth of capital, the social gulf that separates the worker from the capitalist increases at the same time, and the power of capital over labour, the dependence of labour on capital, likewise increases at the same time.[43]

In terms of envy and the social psychology of wealth, the notion of relative wages rings true. But it cuts two ways. Workers may compare themselves not just against their bosses, but also with the absolutely poor. There are usually some people relative to whom they are well off.

Assessment

Marx often saw things in terms of stark opposites: a capitalist market (run by the bourgeoisie) *or* collective planning (by workers). He apparently envisaged that there would be a market in the socialist phase immediately after capitalism. But he did not anticipate that 'market socialism', a pragmatic mixture of individual enterprise and social organisation, could be a long-term, stable and prosperous mode of production. A mixed economy of this kind would combine the dynamism of free enterprise and the discipline of competition with the virtues of strategic planning and cooperation. It would involve a partnership between the market – as a good, flexible, self-adjusting way to allocate resources – and the state which would provide social care, education and environmental regulation, as well as investing in longer-term research and preventing massive unemployment.

Most countries now accept a role for both private, profit-driven enterprise and public 'people-first' services. The market and the state co-exist. Political debate is largely about the balance between the two, and where to set the boundaries between them. The Right advocates tax cuts and less state spending; while the Left gives more support to social services and the public sector.

In this context, Marx's writings about theories of value are anachronistic. But his attempt to relate structured inequality to labour time is still impressive, even if prices cannot be derived from it. And his writing is still stimulating in the way it links the 'economic' with things technological, social and political. In this respect his record of prognostications is much better than often supposed. He accurately predicted:

- the continued spread of the capitalist mode of production across the globe;
- incessant technological progress;

- the ever-growing importance of fixed capital (plant and equipment);
- increasing concentration of wealth;
- a tendency towards buy-outs and monopoly;
- continuation of recurrent business cycles (patterns of 'boom and bust');
- continued pressures to drive wages down (in order to maximise profits); casualisation of labour.

Questions

1. Explain Marx's idea of 'surplus value'. How does it relate to his theory of social class?
2. Would it be possible, or desirable, to organise society without money?
3. What is exploitation? How would you set about defining and analysing it?
4. Is economics as important as Marx thought?
5. 'The car is the Western consumer object. It's the object of expense and wealth. And that's why cars are so important to the kids who steal them. They say everything to me about consumerism and capitalism' (Paul Anderson, director of *Shopping*, a film about joy-riding and ram-raiding). What do cars tell us about consumerism?
6. What would be the optimum combination of free market enterprise and collective planning?

CHAPTER 12

Engels

The Man

1820   Born, to affluent, pious mill-owners in the Rhineland. Eldest of eight children.
Still in his teens, publishes poetry and journalism.
Joins the radical Young Hegelian philosophers.
Calls for Republican government and freedom of the press.

Early 1840s Does military service. Works for the family firm in Manchester, a city of machinery and steam and a major new industrial centre in the world.

By 1842   Influenced by the communism of Moses Hess, calls for radical social reform.

1843   Writes 'Outlines of a Critique of Political Economy'. It is published, 1844, in a journal edited by Marx, who later praises it as a 'brilliant essay'.[1]

1844   Writes *The Condition of the Working Class in England*, based on contemporary documents and his own experience of Manchester. He had been shown around by Mary Burns, an Irish mill-worker, whom he lived with.

August 1844 Meets Marx in Paris.

1845–46   Collaborates with Marx on *The Holy Family* and *The German Ideology*. These promote what they call 'materialism' and attack the 'idealism' of the Young Hegelians.
Also occupied with political agitation and education among German artisans in Paris and Brussels.
Not that life was all grim. 'If I had an income of 5,000 francs I would do nothing but work and amuse myself with women until I went to pieces. If there were no Frenchwomen, life wouldn't be worth living.'[2]

1847–48   Drafts a first version of the *Communist Manifesto*.

1848   Contributes many articles to the newspaper Marx was editing in Cologne (the *Neue Rheinische Zeitung*, suppressed May 1849).

1848–49	Joins in armed uprisings by workers in southern Germany. After their failure, he sails from Genoa to London, to join Marx in exile.
1850–69	Works for the family firm in Manchester, 'accursed commerce'.[3] Even at work, he enjoys poetry, beer, cigars and a snooze after lunch in his hammock.

Regularly sends Marx money. Moves in both proletarian and bourgeois circles. Goes fox-hunting with the Cheshire Hunt.[4]

Writes articles for the *New York Daily Tribune*, in Marx's name. These include (1851–52) a series on 'Revolution and Counter-revolution in Germany', about the abortive 1848–49 revolutions. He links their failure to the uprisings of the sixteenth century, in 'The Peasant War in Germany'.

Though busy in the family firm, still writes about military affairs, the Crimean War – and an extensive history of Ireland.

1859	Circulates favourable reviews of Marx's *Contribution to the Critique of Political Economy*. Praises what he calls Marx's 'dialectical method' and his 'materialist conception of history'.
1863	Engels' common-law wife, Mary Burns, dies suddenly. Engels has his one and only breach with Marx, who offered the briefest condolences, before bemoaning his own financial problems (no shoes for the children). He added, tastelessly: 'instead of Mary, ought it not to have been my mother, who is in any case a prey to physical ailments and has had her fair share of life...?' Engels was offended by this 'frosty' letter, but they soon made up.[5]
1867	Writes anonymous reviews of *Capital*, comparing Marx's achievement with Darwin's.
1870	'Retires' and comes to live near Marx in London. Pays off Marx's outstanding debts and gives him an allowance of £350 per annum.[6]

Engels looks after Marx. 'The fact is that I cannot bear to be without a lot of exercise out of doors and, whether he wants to or not, Marx mostly has to come along with me, and that is after all the best medicine for him.'[7]

Engels' family never approved of Marx. He tried to explain it to his mother. 'If Marx were not here, or did not even exist, it would make absolutely no difference at all. It is therefore quite wrong to put the blame on him. Incidentally, I can also remember the time when

Marx's relations maintained that *I* had been the ruin of him.'[8]

Engels' interest in the origins of words led him to study at least 25 languages, including Dutch Frisian and Celtic Irish.[9]

1874	Publishes 'On Authority', against Bakunin and the anarchists. Argues that large-scale industry will need some authority and subordination, even after revolution.
1876	Writes *Dialectics of Nature*. (First pub. 1927.) He tries to present Marxism as a science; and to appropriate the status and credibility of natural science for Marxism.
1878	Publishes *Anti-Dühring*, just before Bismarck's anti-socialist laws impose censorship in Germany. Three chapters are later published in ...
1880	*Socialism: Utopian and Scientific*. These works do more than any other to popularise Marxism.
1883	Marx dies.
1883–95	Engels becomes the spokesman for Marxism, or, it might be said, invents Marxism. Corresponds with socialist leaders across the world. Edits and publishes Marx's manuscripts. Writes prefaces and introductions to new editions of Marx's works. Edits *Capital*, Volumes II and III.
1884	Publishes *Origin of the Family, Private Property and the State*. It is based on the work of Lewis Henry Morgan, whose study of Native American culture, *Ancient Society*, came out in 1877. Engels uses this, Marx's notes on it and further material on Greece, Rome, Celts and Germans.
1888	*Ludwig Feuerbach and the End of Classical German Philosophy*. Argues that Marx used and improved on the materialism of Feuerbach and the dialectics of Hegel.
1895	Dies. Leaves most of his money to Marx's daughters. Ashes scattered in the English Channel, off Beachy Head.

A Warrant of Arrest, 1849

Description: 1. *Engels*. Age 26 to 28; height 5 feet 6 inches; hair blond; forehead smooth; eyebrows blond; eyes blue; nose and mouth well proportioned; beard reddish; chin oval; face oval;

complexion healthy; figure slender. Special characteristics: speaks very rapidly and is short-sighted ... .[10]

A 'Confession', 1868

Written by Engels in the notebook of Marx's daughter Jenny, this shows the more informal side of the man.[11]

Table 12.1: Engels' entry in Jenny Marx's notebook

Your favourite virtue	jollity
Favourite quality	
– in man	to mind his own business
– in woman	not to mislay things
Chief characteristic	knowing everything by halves
Idea of happiness	Château Margaux 1848[a]
Idea of misery	to go to a dentist
The vice you excuse	excess of any sort
The vice you detest	Cant
Your aversion	affected stuck up woman
Characters you most dislike	Spurgeon
Favourite occupation	chaffing and being chaffed
– Hero	none
– Heroine	too many to name one
– Poet	Reineke de Vos,[b] Shakespeare, Ariosto, etc.
– Prose Writer	Goethe, Lessing, Dr Samelson
– Flower	Blue Bell
– Colour	any one not Aniline
– Dish	Cold: Salad, hot: Irish Stew
– Maxim	not to have any
– Motto	take it aisy

[a] Vintage wine from the year of Revolution.
[b] 'Reynard the Fox'.

Assessment

What I contributed – at any rate with the exception of my work in a few special fields – Marx could very well have done without me. What Marx accomplished I would not have achieved. Marx stood higher, saw further, and took a wider and quicker view than all the rest of us. Marx was a genius; we others were at best talented.[12]

Engels' writing tends to be clearer than Marx's. He is more accessible and even. He had a gift for popularising complex ideas in lucid, classical prose. In his life he seems better organised than Marx, with great self-discipline and an impressive ability to ignore distractions and achieve priorities.[13] His work always appears measured and planned. Marx is more irregular, inconsistent, startling, prone to digress, or stumble unexpectedly on a new insight, contrasting detail and longer view. Marx explores; Engels explains.

By the age of 24, Engels had probably achieved more than Marx. He had made the leap from Hegelian philosophy to social critique and political economy. His 'Outlines of a Critique of Political Economy' (1843) anticipate much of Marx's later work. His *Condition of the Working Class in England* (1844) combines empirical detail and social observation. Although he attributes the materialist conception of history to Marx, he himself played an important role as catalyst or support. In the 1850s and 1860s, his financial aid kept the Marx family alive.

When Engels returned to his own research, he was too keen to find 'scientific laws' and to turn Marx's diverse thoughts into a unified system. The would-be 'positivist' in him triumphed over the critical thinker. He looked for real laws in nature, society and science; as if social science could adopt the method of natural science and discover social laws.

Dialectics is best understood as an interesting method of enquiry, a conceptual tool kit, but Engels is not content to leave it at that. He defines dialectics as 'the science of the general laws of motion, both of the external world and of human thinking'.[14] These 'laws', attributed by Engels to Hegel, 'can be reduced in the main to three':

1. the law of the transformation of quantity into quality and vice versa;
2. the law of the interpenetration of opposites;
3. the law of the negation of the negation.[15]

Engels thinks these 'are real laws of development of nature, and therefore are valid also for theoretical natural science'.[16] His attempt to illustrate these 'laws' is as bizarre as it is brilliant. He tried to draw general conclusions from contemporary scientific advances, notably evolution; the transformation of energy; and the discovery of the cell as the basic unit of living organisms. Later Marxists – notably Plekhanov, Lenin and his followers – believed that Engels *had* discovered new laws and perfected a *science* of dialectics. For them, Engels' work on dialectics is 'an act of historic importance'. Others might describe it as 'mysticism and incomprehensible transcendentalism'; or else say that to the extent it is rational, it is merely pointing out 'something quite self-evident, trivial and commonplace'.[17] There is a probably unavoidable element of dogmatism in Engels' claim to have discovered all-encompassing laws. Where he announces 'laws' and 'proofs', we would speak only of patterns, examples and illustrations.

The saving grace in Engels is his extraordinary openness and effusive interest in all areas of scientific research. The scale of his project is both ill-advised and awesome. In *Dialectics of Nature*, for instance, he ranges irrepressibly across, amongst other things, spiritualism, tidal friction, heat, electricity, the part played by labour in the transition from ape to man, mathematics, mechanics, astronomy, physics, chemistry and biology.

CHAPTER 13

Marx and Gender

This chapter
- begins with Engels, whose thinking about gender is more extensive than that of Marx;
- looks at Marx's personal life and the 'sexual politics' he lived by;
- cites some of his comments on the family and on conditions faced by working-class women;
- shows how some of his key ideas have been adapted and developed by feminists;
- looks at the 'Wages for Housework' movement and the debate about domestic labour;
- argues that, despite the overlap, feminism is ultimately incompatible with (existing) Marxism; and offers an important critique of Marxism.

Engels' View

> Within the family, [the husband] is the bourgeois, and the wife represents the proletariat.[1]

The words are Engels' and the implications are extensive. For if the husband 'is the bourgeois', this suggests that what Marx and Engels wrote about power and inequality with respect to class should equally be applied to gender.

Engels wanted to explain the rise of male power (patriarchy), which he thought was connected to the growth of private property. He believed that originally things had been more equal. The early human tribe, or *gens*, would have been organised in a large household, as a kind of 'primitive communism'. Descent and inheritance were reckoned by the mother's line, not the father's. The work done by women was valued as much as the men's work. This changed when tribes broke up into monogamous families. Instead of doing public and social work, women were reduced to servicing their husbands.

> The overthrow of mother-right was the world-historical defeat of the female sex. The man took command in the home also; the woman was degraded and reduced to servitude; she became

the slave of his lust and a mere instrument for the production of children.[2]

Engels' view of the past stemmed from very limited evidence, as did everyone else's at the time. He was basing his account on the work of the American anthropologist, Lewis Henry Morgan, whose *Ancient Society* appeared in 1877.

Marx the Man: a Chauvinist?

In many ways and by modern, liberal standards, Marx was quite chauvinist. He hoped for sons rather than daughters.[3] His own family life was fairly conventional. He fathered a child, whom he did not visit or acknowledge, by the family servant. He once wrote, in a parlour game, that his favourite virtue in woman was weakness. Generally, he had a romantic, Victorian view of women. His wife, self-sacrificing and dedicated to socialist ideals, subscribed to traditional, patriarchal assumptions about the role of women (service, 'modesty and maidenly good manners').[4] She accepted the conventional role of women, but was frustrated by it.

> In all these struggles we women have the harder part to bear, because it is the lesser one. A man draws strength from his struggle with the world outside, and is invigorated by the sight of the enemy, be their number legion. We remain sitting at home, darning socks. That does nothing to dispel our fears and the gnawing day-to-day petty worries slowly but surely sap our spirit. I can say this from over 30 years' experience, and can certainly claim that I am not one to lose heart easily.[5]

An International Women's Association, demanding equal rights for women, was set up in 1868. It was chaired by Marie Goegg. Marx calls her 'Madame General Geck', where Geck means 'dandy' or 'fop'. His tone is jocular and patronising.

> Tell your dear wife that I never 'suspected' her of serving under Madame General Geck. I queried only in jest. Incidentally, the ladies cannot complain about the *'International'*, since it has appointed a lady, Madame Law, as a member of the *General Council*. Joking aside, very great progress was demonstrated at the last congress of the American *'LABOR UNION'*, inter alia, by the fact that it treated the women workers with full parity; by contrast, the English, and to an even greater extent the gallant French, are displaying a marked narrowness of spirit in this respect. Everyone who knows anything of history also knows that great social revolutions are impossible without the feminine ferment. Social progress may be measured precisely by the social position of the fair sex (plain ones included).[6]

Note the attitudinal swings even in this one paragraph. First the question of the 'ladies' is laughed off. Then Marx seems to become serious, praising the American Unions and noting the role of the 'feminine ferment', although that metaphor should perhaps warn us. At the end, he undercuts it all with a cheap, patriarchal 'joke'.

It would be wrong and anachronistic to portray Marx as a complete chauvinist. Indeed, by the standards of his time, he might just pass as a progressive on gender issues. At least he ensured that his daughters had a good education. He was not a sexual revolutionary and, apart from the vision of communism, he did nothing to advocate alternative lifestyles. And the tendency of Marxist states was to maintain the family as institution, backed up by nurseries and publicly available child care; and to send women to work with men on more equal terms in the public domain, but not to encourage men to work in the home.

Writings on Family and Gender

In terms of his work, Marx was focused on power at the 'macro' level: class conflict, the battles between large groups. He underestimated the importance of 'micro' power, such as one-to-one or small-scale power struggles. He neglected all the ways in which 'the personal is political'. He did not theorise about gender as such and how it fits in ('articulates') with the concept of class. That was not an issue for him. His wider thinking on equality of the sexes is almost non-existent, especially compared with his contemporary, John Stuart Mill, or August Bebel, whose *Woman under Socialism* (1883) became the most read socialist tract in the German language.

That said, there is in Marx's work rather more about marriage, the family and the sexual division of labour than is usually supposed. (The 'sexual division of labour' refers to divisions in the work-force, for example, how women often get low-paid, traditionally feminine jobs to do with cleaning, caring, preparing or serving food.) We will be looking at short passages and incidental comments which are left undeveloped.

'Under the dominion of private property and money', Marx wrote, 'the species-relation itself, the relation between man and woman etc., becomes an object of trade! The woman is bought and sold.'[7] Rather than follow this up, he continues to discuss commerce, Christianity and Judaism.

Marx calls marriage 'certainly a *form of exclusive private property*'. But this is peripheral to his main interests, as evident in the sentence below.

Prostitution is only a specific expression of the general prostitution of the labourer, and since it is a relationship in which falls not the prostitute alone, but also the one who prostitutes – and the latter's abomination is still greater – the capitalist, etc., also comes under this head.[8]

Marx goes on to say that 'the direct, natural and necessary relationship of person to person is the *relation of man to woman* ... . From this relationship one can therefore judge man's whole level of development.'[9] He is here following Fourier's formulation: 'The degree of emancipation of woman is the natural measure of general emancipation.'[10] He approves of Fourier's 'masterly characterisation of marriage' as double prostitution and writes that 'the general position of women in modern society is inhuman',[11] but again does not pursue the idea.

Marx realises that the 'private' and the 'public' spheres influence each other. People cannot simply punch out and leave their thoughts and feelings at the work-place. Abuse at work spawns abuse at home.

The most cowardly, unresisting people become implacable as soon as they can exercise their absolute parental authority. The abuse of this authority is, as it were, a crude compensation for all the submissiveness and dependence to which they abase themselves willy-nilly in bourgeois society.[12]

The German Ideology speaks of 'the slavery latent in the family';[13] and asserts that in the family, the 'wife and children are slaves of the husband'.[14] It describes marriage, property and the family as 'the practical basis on which the bourgeoisie has erected its domination' and 'the conditions which make the bourgeois a bourgeois'. In the bourgeois family 'boredom and money are the binding link' and 'its dirty existence has its counterpart in the holy concept of it in official phraseology and universal hypocrisy'. For the proletariat, 'the concept of the family does not exist at all, but here and there family affection based on extremely real relations is certainly to be found'. In the French Revolution, the family was for a time 'as good as legally abolished', but it remained in practice, because the mode of production required 'the real body of the family, the property relation, the exclusive attitude in relation to other families, forced cohabitation – relations determined by the existence of children, the structure of modern towns, the formation of capital, etc.'.[15] This is edging towards a history and sociology of the family, though Marx characteristically veers away to tilt at the bourgeoisie.

The 'Theses on Feuerbach' proclaim that 'once the earthly family is discovered to be the secret of the holy family, the former must then itself be criticised in theory and transformed in practice'.[16]

> 'Abolition of the family!' Even the most radical flare up at this infamous proposal of the Communists.
> On what foundation is the present family, the bourgeois family, based? On capital, on private gain. In its completely developed form this family exists only among the bourgeoisie. But this state of things finds its complement in the practical absence of the family among the proletarians, and in public prostitution.[17]

'Abolition of the family!' The German word is *'Aufhebung'*, a Hegelian term, which suggests not mere destruction, but also a building up on a higher level. Marx probably had in mind the *'Aufhebung'* of the family based merely on financial self-interest, in favour of a family where people live together from their own free will, out of true human affection. If this was his position, it is characteristic that he did not make it absolutely clear. His comments in the *Manifesto* are more like slogans than considered reflections and he seems more concerned with attacking the bourgeoisie than thinking about sexual inequality *per se*. Likewise, although Marx and Engels criticise the rhetorical, romantic 'cult of the female' and talk instead of looking at the 'present social position of women', they themselves are at the time scoring points rather than saying anything constructive about women and gender.[18]

In *Capital*, Marx suggests that originally the division of labour is biologically based.

> Within a family and, after further development, within a tribe, there springs up naturally a division of labour caused by differences of sex and age, and therefore based on a purely physiological foundation.[19]

He describes the conditions faced by working-class women and condemns the hypocrisy and heartlessness of employers.

> Before the labour of women and children under 10 years old was forbidden in mines, the capitalists considered the employment of naked women and girls, often in company with men, so far sanctioned by their moral code, and especially by their ledgers, that it was only after the passing of the [Factory] Act that they had recourse to machinery ... . In England women are still occasionally used instead of horses for hauling barges ... .[20]

In the light of modern theories of gender, this simple description of over-work and oppression, with almost no theoretical elaboration, seems unsophisticated. Nonetheless the unpretentious, empirical style points us towards similar and similarly forgotten facts today – the lives of women exploited in sweatshops, or working long hours assembling micro-chips.

Marx tends to discuss women's paid work in the same context as the employment of children, as if the two are similar or comparable. He was concerned that the contemporary factory system was sacrificing women and children, as it undoubtedly was, but he makes the dubious assumption that male workers are more likely to be militant.

> There can be no doubt that the factory system sacrifices women and children more than any other system. Moreover, the preponderance of women and children in the mechanical workshops breaks the *resistance* [of the workers] and adds a passive element which also condemns the adults to slavery, to passive subordination.[21]

His attitude to the over-work of women has a slightly chivalric tone. He wants women 'to be rigorously excluded from *all nightwork* whatever, and all sort of work hurtful to the delicacy of the sex, or exposing their bodies to poisonous or otherwise deleterious agencies'.[22] He regrets that 'the capitalist mode of exploitation, by sweeping away the economic foundation which corresponded to parental power, made the use of parental power into its misuse'.[23] But he is optimistic about future prospects; for, in giving work to women, young people and children, large-scale industry creates 'a new economic foundation for a higher form of the family and of relations between the sexes'.

> It is also obvious that the fact that the collective working group is composed of individuals of both sexes and all ages must under the appropriate conditions turn into a source of humane development, although in its spontaneously developed, brutal, capitalist form, the system works in the opposite direction, and becomes a pestiferous source of corruption and slavery, since here the worker exists for the process of production, and not the process of production for the worker.[24]

Marx's primary interest is in economic theory, as illustrated by the following sentence. 'Women in ancient domestic industry, for instance, produced coats without producing the exchange value of coats.'[25] He wants to make a neat theoretical point, not to write an historical or experiential account of gender. When he does make radical sounds about the family, the impression is that he is not wholly serious, that he enjoys being *enfant terrible* and *bête noire*, scandalising the bourgeoisie.

Applying Marx to Gender

Notwithstanding all this, some feminists have used and developed some of Marx's ideas about alienation, ideology and exploitation; his materialist approach; and his emphasis on economic relations and the social construction of identity.

The materialist conception of history takes the focus away from traditional men's history ('the biography of great men') and on to everyday life and the daily reproduction of essentials. Marx wants to study 'real individuals, their activity and the material conditions of their life'.[26] His first premise is that

> men must be in a position to live in order to be able to 'make history'. But life involves before everything else eating and drinking, housing, clothing and various other things.[27]

The second point Marx notes is the creation of new needs. The third is the reproduction of family and social life. It is perhaps because all this seems to mark up the historical role of women that the word 'men' stands out as anomalous and sexist.

> The third circumstance which, from the very outset, enters into historical development, is that men, who daily recreate their own life, begin to make other men, to propagate their kind: the relation between man and woman, parents and children, the *family*.[28]

Marx insisted that what we think of as 'completely natural' is often the product of society and thus open to change. We are, he emphasises, social constructs, 'the ensemble of the social relations'.[29] In this sense, he perhaps contributed something to the general distinction between nature and culture, which was later used by the women's movement to differentiate 'sex' and 'gender'.

Table 13.1: Distinction between nature and culture

Nature	Culture
'Sex'	'Gender'
Innate	Socialised
Natural	Conditioned
Biology	Humanities
Female	Feminine
Male	Masculine
Unchangeable	Changeable

The first column concerns those differences which are innate and anatomical. This is studied by biology and the words 'male' and 'female' apply. Other differences, commonly taken to be 'natural', may to a large extent be socially constructed. This would mean that women and men have the potential to be other than they are. Gender differences (in areas like work, family and behaviour) are the proper study of the humanities and social sciences.

Marx's method could be used to analyse the 'private', family sphere ('relations of reproduction') rather than only the public, economic sphere ('relations of production'). One can change his categories and reverse his priorities, but retain something of his language and approach.

> The sexual-reproductive organisation of society always furnishes the real basis, starting from which we can alone work out the ultimate explanation of the whole superstructure of economic, juridical and political institutions as well as of the religious, philosophical and other ideas of a given historical period.[30]

Socialist feminists have applied Marx's method in a way which is creative and political, academic and populist, to examine the subordination of women in the sexual division of labour, segmentation of the labour market and property rights.

Wages for Housework and the 'Domestic Labour Debate'

In the 1970s and 1980s there was a vigorous debate about women's work, paid and unpaid. One participant was Selma James, who refines some undeveloped nuggets in Marx's work, to explore the question of domestic labour. He had noted that 'the maintenance and reproduction of the working class remains a necessary condition for the reproduction of capital'.[31] It requires 'the transmission and accumulation of skills from one generation to another'. He called this 'Simple Reproduction', the title of Chapter 23 in *Capital*.[32] James shows that this process of reproduction, essential to capitalism, corresponds to what we now call 'unwaged work', 'women's work'. It is this unpaid housework which reproduces the worker every morning in a fit state to work; and which brings up fresh, new workers to replace those who are finished off. Unwaged work produces the goose that lays the golden egg. It produces labour power.

> This is a strange commodity for it is not a thing. The ability to labour resides only in a human being whose life is consumed in the process of producing. First it must be nine months in the womb, must be fed, clothed, trained. Then when it works, its bed must be made, its floors swept, its lunchbox prepared, its sexuality not gratified but quietened, its dinner ready when it gets home even if this is eight in the morning from the night shift. This is how labour power is produced and reproduced

when it is daily consumed in the factory or the office. To describe its basic production and reproduction is to describe women's work.[33]

James and the group 'Wages for Housework' argue that those who do this 'invisible work' should be both valued and paid. This could be done by increasing Child Benefit, Income Support including for single parents, pensions for older women, benefits for women with disabilities, etc.

Selma James follows Marx in that she sees women's work as being mainly for the benefit of capital. Others (including Engels at times) stress that women's work is for the benefit of men.[34] All men are bought off by being able to control at least some women. The question at the heart of the 'domestic labour debate' in the 1970s and early 1980s was: do women work mainly for capital or mainly for men? Marxists stressed the former and feminists the latter. The answer is probably both; in which case the real problem is to say which is more significant in any given circumstance. The debate was linked to the wider one of whether patriarchy precedes capitalism (a feminist position) or whether (as some Marxists argued) the two arose together.

Assessment

Marxists often tried to subsume feminism under a class analysis and to colonise or co-opt it for their own ends, to inject life into their own moribund movement. The most successful branches of feminism were those which had least to do with Marxism. Liberal feminism concentrated on equal rights for women, equal opportunities, child care provision and the role of law and education in increasing women's choices. And 'radical' or 'separatist' feminism looks at everyday behaviour, focusing on male violence, male control of female sexuality and reproduction and male invasions of women's issues. It offers a far-reaching critique of the overall approach or mind-set of Marxism, which was profoundly masculine in its

- emphasis on struggle;
- attempts to control others;
- macho posturing;
- tendency to be aggressive and confrontational;
- obsessive intellectualism, the theoretical equivalent of trainspotting;
- exclusion of others through technical language and hairsplitting debates about arcane topics;
- unwillingness to discuss emotions, based on a superficial contempt (or fear) of the 'softer' emotions;
- neglect of nurturance, sharing and growth.

All of these limitations are already there in Marx. Contrasting his writings with those of his wife reveals an emotional division of labour of a depressingly conventional kind. Karl is forceful, aggressive, assured: Jenny is caring, worrying, nurturing. After the massacre of the Communards, Jenny laments:[35] Karl rallies the troops.[36] His is a 'man's job'. He attacks 'womanish resignation';[37] and mocks others as 'old women'.[38] He writes as a man – a clever, forceful man – unaware of how this restricts his impact and his range.

Marx assumes that production is the only or main source of oppression; and that true happiness has to do with the creative labour of artistic expression – when clearly more people find it in loving relationships. These assumptions seem distinctively male ones. The central categories of Marxism are sex-blind. And the typically masculine culture of Marxism alienates many who might otherwise be sympathetic.

Marx and his followers spurned the language for exploring doubt, insecurity, vulnerability. This entails a loss of openness and a diminished capacity to learn from errors, to listen to criticism and to grow. Marxism hardened into a narrowly masculine mind-set: political belligerence and intellectual cock-sureness, masking deeper insecurity. The need to be right and to put others in the wrong precipitates destructive in-fighting and faction-forming, periodic purges and regular accusations of foul play, along with vicious denunciations of supposed traitors. Marxism lacks the necessary perspectives to make sense of this.

Questions

1. 'Within the family, [the husband] is the bourgeois, and the wife represents the proletariat.' What did Engels mean? Was he right?
2. 'The emancipation of woman will only be possible when woman can take part in production on a large, social scale, and domestic work no longer claims anything but an insignificant amount of her time' (Engels). What else would women's liberation involve?
3. What are the main issues concerning gender today? Can Marxism contribute anything to understanding or resolving them?
4. Is the relationship between Marxism and feminism a natural union or a forced marriage?
5. 'Abolition of the family.' What could this mean? Is it (a) possible? (b) desirable?
6. What are the alternatives to living in families? What are the advantages and disadvantages of these alternatives?

CHAPTER 14

Colonialism

This chapter cites Marx's writings on

- nationalism as a divisive force in the working class;
- the globalisation of capitalism;
- the Opium Wars in China;
- India and other colonies;
- Ireland;
- how colonial and slave labour support class exploitation in Europe.

It then looks at Lenin's theory of imperialism and unjust aspects of the world economy today.

Class, Nationalism and Racism

Class struggle is central to Marx's thought. But the English working class was not as united nor as militant as Marx hoped. One reason for this was nationalism ...

> And most important of all! All industrial and commercial centres in England now have a working class divided into two hostile camps, English PROLETARIANS and Irish PROLETARIANS. The ordinary English worker hates the Irish worker as a competitor who forces down the STANDARD OF LIFE. In relation to the Irish worker, he feels himself to be a member of the ruling nation and, therefore, makes himself a tool of his aristocrats and capitalists against Ireland, thus strengthening their domination over himself. He harbours religious, social and national prejudices against him. His attitude towards him is roughly that of the poor WHITES to the NIGGERS in the former slave states of the American Union. The Irishman PAYS HIM BACK WITH INTEREST IN HIS OWN MONEY. He sees in the English worker both the accomplice and the stupid tool of English rule in Ireland.[1]

The letter goes on to discuss the role of the press, the pulpit and the comic papers in fuelling antagonism between English and Irish workers. It implies that racism stems from collective economic self-interest. Economic insecurity breeds compensating feelings of superiority and the cherishing of prejudices, which are then reciprocated by the other group. The oppressors dismiss their victims as inferior or sub-human, perhaps as a way of repressing any feelings of guilt. Later Marxists have argued that racism is a product of our colonial past. It is the ideology of imperialism.

Marx himself did *not* fully explore racism. Clearly it has something to do with suspicion and fear (of other beliefs, other values, other cultures) and something to do with ignorance – not understanding others. Marx occasionally descended to racist slurs, particularly against his rival Lassalle, whom he abused as a 'Jewish Nigger'.[2] Several anti-Semitic comments suggest that he was insecure about his own Jewish background. And he was deeply prejudiced against the Slavs. On a more positive note, Marx did support the abolition of slavery in the United States and the emancipation of the serfs in Russia, describing these two movements as 'the most momentous thing happening in the world today'.[3]

Globalisation of Capitalism

His writing does shed light on colonialism and the historical background to racism. He especially emphasised that capitalism is an inherently expansive system. In his time, it did not cover the globe. He predicted, accurately, that it soon would.

> The bourgeoisie, by the rapid improvement of all instruments of production, by the immensely facilitated means of communication, draws all, even the most barbarian, nations into civilisation. The cheap prices of its commodities are the heavy artillery with which it batters down all Chinese walls, with which it forces the barbarians' intensely obstinate hatred of foreigners to capitulate. It compels all nations, on pain of extinction, to adopt the bourgeois mode of production; it compels them to introduce what it calls civilisation into their midst, i.e., to become bourgeois themselves. In one word, it creates a world after its own image.[4]

The word 'barbarian' seems prejudiced, but Marx does not wholly subscribe to a dichotomy of civilised people and barbarians. He puts a question mark under the meaning of 'civilisation' by using the phrase 'what it calls civilisation'. He sees capitalism as dynamic and expansionist, speaking of 'the law which gives capital no rest and continually whispers in its ear: "Go on! Go on!"'[5]

Long before the enormous multinational corporations of our own time, Marx foresaw that industry was becoming *globalised*.

> Thanks to the machine, the spinner can live in England while the weaver resides in the East Indies. Before the invention of

machinery, the industry of a country was carried on chiefly with raw materials that were the products of its own soil; in England – wool, in Germany – flax, in France – silks and flax, in the East Indies and the Levant – cotton, etc. Thanks to the application of machinery and of steam, the division of labour was able to assume such dimensions that large-scale industry, detached from the national soil, depends entirely on the world market, on international exchange, on an international division of labour.[6]

Marx set out to analyse the consequences of the expansion of capitalism. His initial idea was to write six books.

(1) Capital. (2) Landed Property. (3) Wage Labour. (4) The State. (5) International Trade. (6) World Market.[7]

In the event Marx managed only the first part of this plan. But in his articles on the expansion of capitalism, he did describe some of the horrors of colonialism. His journalism about China, for instance, examines events during and after the first Opium War (1839–42) and the second Opium War (1856–58).

Colonialism and Revolution

Disappointed by the defeat of the 1848 uprisings in Europe, Marx toyed with the idea of revolution in the East preceding that in the West.[8] In 1853 he was hopefully predicting that 'the Chinese revolution will throw the spark into the overloaded mine of the present industrial system and cause the explosion of the long-prepared general crisis, which, spreading abroad, will be closely followed by political revolutions on the Continent'.[9]

Marx wrote many articles about India, 'that great and interesting country', with titles such as

- The British Rule in India;
- The East India Company – Its History and Results;
- The Government of India;
- The Future Results of the British Rule in India;
- The Revolt in the Indian Army;
- Investigation of Tortures in India;
- British Incomes in India;
- Taxes in India;
- The Indian Bill.

He believed that colonialism was 'dragging individuals and peoples through blood and dirt, through misery and degradation', but balanced this with an optimistic view of the future.

Bourgeois industry and commerce create these material conditions of a new world in the same way as geological revolutions have created the surface of the earth. When a great social revolution shall have mastered the results of the bourgeois epoch, the market of the world and the modern powers of production, and subjected them to the common control of the most advanced peoples, then only will human progress cease to resemble that hideous pagan idol, who would not drink the nectar but from the skulls of the slain.[10]

The final image, picturesque and grotesque, evokes the image of pagans and idols – and all the cultural prejudice involved in that – but gives the idea a twist, suggesting that 'progress' is the real idol, and 'civilisation' barbarism. Marx apparently envisages that after the revolution, 'the most advanced peoples' are still in charge, albeit socialistically in charge.

In other articles Marx and Engels wrote about the effects of colonialism on Burma, Persia, Afghanistan, Algeria and the Ionian Islands. They had a particular interest in Ireland and English misrule there.

Ireland is the bulwark of the *English landed aristocracy*. The exploitation of that country is not only one of the main sources of this aristocracy's material welfare; it is its greatest *moral* strength ... . Ireland is therefore the great means by which the English aristocracy maintains *its domination in England itself.*[11]

It followed that:

The English working class will *never accomplish anything* BEFORE IT HAS GOT RID OF IRELAND. The lever must be applied in Ireland.[12]

The colony could, then, matter more politically than the metropolis. Marx and Engels insisted on an ultimate unity of interest between the workers within the colonial powers and the workers in the colonies. They upheld internationalism and solidarity. Witness their response to the American Civil War. The English cotton owners wanted England to intervene on the side of the slave-owners of the American South ('the Confederacy') in order to maintain cheap supplies of cotton from the black slaves there. Marx and other workers opposed this. They supported the North ('the Union'), even though the price was unemployment and misery for workers in England. Marx spoke of the 'criminal folly' of the ruling classes, who wanted to plunge 'headlong into an infamous crusade for the perpetuation and propagation of slavery on the other side of the Atlantic'. And he praised the 'heroic resistance' of the working class to this 'criminal folly'.[13]

Marx emphasised the similarity between slavery and wage labour and argued that the former was a prerequisite for the latter.

Direct slavery is just as much the pivot of bourgeois industry as machinery, credits, etc. Without slavery you have no cotton; without cotton you have no modern industry. It is slavery that gave the colonies their value; it is the colonies that created world trade, and it is world trade that is the pre-condition of large-scale industry. Thus slavery is an economic category of the greatest importance.[14]

More than most modern sociologists, Marx is aware of the importance of the international division of labour and the role of colonial and slave labour in propping up the class system in Europe.

While the cotton industry introduced child-slavery into England, in the United States it gave the impulse for the transformation of the earlier, more or less patriarchal slavery into a system of commercial exploitation. In fact the veiled slavery of the wage-labourers in Europe needed the unqualified slavery of the New World as its pedestal.[15]

Marx wanted to analyse the economic relationship between coloniser and colonised, between capitalism and poverty. He used the word 'imperialism', but only loosely and did not make much of it.[16] He knew that 'one nation can grow rich at the expense of another' just as 'one class can enrich itself at the expense of another'.[17] The aristocratic Whigs in England could afford lower rent for domestic tenants in England 'because they consider themselves as the heaven-born farmers of the revenues of the British Empire'.[18] Profit repatriated from overseas could be used to cosset and depoliticise the English working class. Engels was especially aware of this.

You ask me what the English workers think about colonial policy. Well, exactly what they think of any policy – the same as what the middle classes think. There is, after all, no labour party here, only conservatives and liberal-radicals, and the workers gaily share the feast of England's monopoly of the world market and the colonies.[19]

Imperialism

This idea – that the English workers were 'sharing the feast' of colonialism – was later developed by Lenin in his booklet *Imperialism: The Highest Stage of Capitalism*. Written at the time of the Russian Revolution, it argued that capitalism had moved into a new phase. This new phase, called 'imperialism', was characterised by (a) 'the partitioning of the world and the exploitation of other countries' and (b) 'high monopoly profits for a handful of very rich countries'. This (c) 'makes it economically possible to bribe the upper strata of the proletariat, and thereby fosters, gives shape to, and strengthens opportunism'.[20]

From the very outset, there is reason to beware of terms such as 'imperialism'. Seemingly analytic concepts can also be loaded terms which pre-judge and condemn the very things they ostensibly study. It may be that the capitalist countries grew rich for quite positive reasons: a lessening of central control and the emergence of a society which allowed unprecedented autonomy, diversity and freedom to experiment.[21] The concept of 'imperialism' allowed Lenin to explain why the advanced industrial countries were thriving; and, at the time of the First World War, to argue that wars were caused by an economic system which is intrinsically war-prone due to conflicts over markets, sources of raw materials, trade routes and investment outlets.

The shift from capitalism to imperialism has something to do with changes in the forces of production. Pure science had converged with mechanical engineering to produce a mass of new products: sophisticated machine tools, the internal combustion engine, pneumatic tyres, aluminium, cars, bikes, phones, typewriters, linoleum, cheap paper, more prefabricated clothes, shoes, etc. New industries sprang up, notably the steel, electricity, chemical and oil industries. All these required massive capital input and large production units. Big Business could exploit all the advantages of superior technology and research, exclusive patents, massive funds, preferential access to supplies and markets, better sales promotion, etc.[22]

'Imperialism', in Lenin's usage, means

- growth of large enterprises;
- concentration of production in monopolies: massive, integrated, industrial and financial firms;
- a new role for banks as providers of finance capital;
- merging between the banks ('finance capital') and the big monopolies ('industrial capital');
- link-ups between the banks and governments;
- export of finance capital, as bank loans, with conditions and stipulations attached;
- 'the export of capital thus becomes a means of encouraging the export of commodities';
- imperialist struggle for the division of the world.

Lenin argued that the real divide was between the rich, colonising countries and the poor, colonised ones. The working classes in the rich countries could be bought off by the profits of imperialism.

The truly revolutionary classes were the poor of what we now call the 'Third World'. Capitalism had singled out 'a handful of exceptionally rich and powerful states', a tenth or a fifth of the inhabitants of the world, parasites who lived off their income from finance capital, shares and dividends.

> Obviously, out of such enormous super-profits (since they are obtained over and above the profits which capitalists squeeze out of the workers of their 'own' country) it is *possible to bribe* the labour leaders and the upper stratum of the labour aristocracy. And that is just what the capitalists of the 'advanced' countries are doing: they are bribing them in a thousand different ways, direct and indirect, overt and covert. This stratum of workers-turned-bourgeois ... are the real *agents of the bourgeoisie in the working-class* movement ... .[23]

With the exception of a few instances noted above, Marx had usually assumed that revolution was most likely in the advanced capitalist countries: France, England, Germany, etc. Now Lenin was arguing that the motor for revolution had moved to the colonies, since the labour movement in the advanced capitalist countries had been 'bought off'. He wanted to root his thesis in Marx's theory. In one article he speaks of 'numerous references by Marx and Engels to the example of the British labour movement'.[24] In fact he musters only two references by Marx to suggest that the British workers have become less militant. But he does provide six references from Engels on the same lines. Only one of these, however, directly links this trend of embourgeoisment to Britain's monopoly of trade (thanks to the Empire). All of Lenin's references are taken from letters by Marx and Engels; it seems that they were aware of working-class embourgeoisment, but never integrated it into their mature theory.

Justice and the World Economy Now

Imperialism, in Lenin's book, roughly equals capitalism at home plus colonialism abroad. It is based on profits at home and 'super-profits' from cheap labour and cheap raw materials abroad. The concept has been further developed by the pan-Africanist leader, Kwame Nkrumah, in his work *Neo-colonialism: The Last Stage of Imperialism*.

Neo-colonialism is imperialism with a face-lift. The rich countries still own strategic assets in their former colonies, whose economies are dominated by multinational companies, run from and headquartered in the rich countries. But the reality of domination is now screened by a facade of independence. Thus the former colony gets its own flag, national anthem, currency and elite (usually educated in the former colonial power); but it is not fully in control of its economy, internal affairs and foreign relationships.

> The result of neo-colonialism is that foreign capital is used for the exploitation rather than for the development of the less developed parts of the world. Investment under neo-colonialism increases rather than decreases the gap between the rich and the poor countries of the world.[25]

Unfair aspects of the global economic system now include:

1. The terms of trade. The prices we pay for sugar, bananas, coffee, cocoa, tea, etc. are too low to provide a living wage for those who harvest them. Only 15 per cent of what we (in the industrial nations) spend on products from the South, goes to the country of origin. The rest goes to rich companies in the North.[26] The ex-colonies still compete with one another in a struggle to deliver food and raw materials to the richer nations at lower and lower prices. The IMF encourages them to increase exports of cash crops. This floods the market, keeping prices low for consumers in the North.

2. Property, Profit, Power. The international terms of trade are not just settled by abstract 'market forces'. They have to do with basic political matters, rooted in history: inequalities of land ownership, property holding, income and power. The key questions here are:

- Who owns the land, factories, mines, power stations, means of transport, banks, insurance companies, newspapers, TV networks, etc.?
- Who does the work?
- Who profits?
- How much profit remains in the local economy?
- How much is repatriated to the richer country and spread around as dividends for share-holders, etc.?
- How much is repatriated as salaries to foreign 'experts', management and consultancy fees?
- How much so-called 'foreign investment' is actually take-over of existing local businesses?

3. Control. Too much power is in the hands of the industrial nations and their club, the OECD (the Organisation for Economic Co-operation and Development). The huge multinational companies (MNCs) move to whatever country offers the cheapest labour and the laxest environmental monitoring. The economy of the ex-colonies is not geared to the needs of the people there, but to the dictates of the world market, largely determined by fluctuations in consumption and production in the OECD countries.

4. *Structural Disadvantage.* The EU puts trade taxes (tariffs) on the import of processed goods. This deters southern countries from developing their own industries to process their products.

5. *Debt.* In the 1970s and 1980s, banks made huge loans to corrupt 'Third World' elites. These did not benefit the poor in these countries. Nonetheless, it is the poor who are now paying for the loans, with interest. This has led to rising food prices, increased unemployment and a cycle of deprivation and disempowerment.

6. *Standards of Living.* The issues here include, on the one hand, high mortality rates, malnutrition and an environment often damaged by monoculture and growth of cash crops for export; on the other, education, health and community prosperity, access to information and improved quality of life and life chances.

Questions

1. Is it true that workers in the rich countries have been de-radicalised by profit from the ex-colonies?
2. (a) Summarise Lenin's thesis of imperialism in one or two sentences.
   (b) What was its historical context?
   (c) Contrast it with an opposing point of view.
   (d) To what extent is the argument correct? In what respects would you agree with it?
   (e) Briefly state grounds for disagreeing with all or part of the argument.
3. 'Marx and his followers wrote about colonialism largely to explain why Revolution had not occurred as they wanted; and to seek hope that it might occur elsewhere.' Discuss.
4. How *does* racism develop?
5. To what extent is racism 'artificially kept alive and intensified by the press, the pulpit, the comic papers, in short, by all the means at the disposal of the ruling classes'?
6. Does racism perpetuate capitalism?
7. 'Much of what Lenin wrote about deep-rooted inequalities in the global economy still holds good today. His mistake was to link such matters to a violent, revolutionary programme which only alienates most people.'
8. Is 'neo-colonialism' a useful concept? or just a pejorative term for something which actually benefits those involved?

CHAPTER 15

Religion

This short chapter examines the reasons for Marx's hostility to religion and the limitations of his thought about religion. It does not discuss the more intriguing aspects of the relationship between Marx and religion, such as whether Marxism itself qualifies as a religion.

Marx's Hostility to Religion

The free-thinking Enlightenment *philosophes*, whom Marx read in his teens, had seen religion as a bastion of ignorance, dogmatism and fear. They thought philosophy would inevitably battle against theology, pitting clear-sighted reason against blind faith; logic against superstition; and freedom against tyranny. In Marx's own time, David Friedrich Strauss subjected the gospels to withering analysis in his *Life of Jesus* (1835). The Young Hegelians were arguing that the divine is that on to which we project our better qualities. Man makes God in his own image. Feuerbach had argued something like this in his *Essence of Christianity* (1841).

By the time he was a student, Marx opposed the Church – then much stronger than now – largely on the grounds that it served to mystify, frighten and confuse the poor, fobbing them off with talk of heaven, instead of explaining the causes of misery and poverty in the here-and-now. It was a metaphysical compensation package for the oppressed. 'It teaches, as religion is bound to teach: submit to authority for *all authority* is from God.'[1] Christianity had become the accomplice of oppression, sure of its victory, but 'not so sure of it as to spurn the aid of the police'.[2]

Wheeled on to legitimise tyrants, religion could be an offence to both decency and logic. When the German king claimed that the hand of God had directly warded off an assassin's bullet, Marx dryly observed that

> even a slight degree of consistent thought will arrive at the false conclusion that God at the same time both guided the hand of the criminal and diverted the bullet away from the king; for how can one presume a one-sided action on the part of God?[3]

If we could only transcend ancient religious prejudices and divisions, we might at last unite around our common humanity.

As soon as jew and Christian recognise that their respective religions are no more than *different stages in the development of the human mind,* different snake skins cast off by *history,* and that *man* is the snake who sloughed them, the relation of jew and Christian is no longer religious but is only a critical, *scientific* and human relation.[4]

Religion – or religious difference – is the snake in the garden. Marx did not see religion as something imposed on the people; it grows directly out of their miseries. It was a question of analysing religion, setting out from the assumption: '*man makes religion,* religion does not make man'.[5]

Religious suffering is at the same time an expression of real suffering and a protest against real suffering. Religion is the sigh of the oppressed creature, the feeling of a heartless world, and the soul of soulless circumstances. It is the opium of the people.

The abolition of religion as the illusory happiness of the people is the demand for their real happiness.[6]

Marx was not just making an intellectual or psychological critique of Christianity. He had developed a deep hatred of it and the way it was being used to keep the poor down. When a Prussian Consistorial Councillor urged people to counter communism by developing 'the social principles of Christianity', Marx fired off this reply:

The social principles of Christianity have now had eighteen hundred years to be developed, and need no further development by Prussian Consistorial Counsellors.

The social principles of Christianity justified the slavery of antiquity, glorified the serfdom of the Middle Ages and are capable, in case of need, of defending the oppression of the proletariat, even if with somewhat doleful grimaces.

The social principles of Christianity preach the necessity of a ruling and an oppressed class, and for the latter all they have to offer is the pious wish that the former may be charitable.

The social principles of Christianity place the Consistorial Councillor's compensation for all infamies in heaven, and thereby justify the further existence of these infamies on earth.

The social principles of Christianity declare all the vile acts of the oppressors against the oppressed to be either a just punishment for original sin and other sins, or trials which the Lord, in his infinite wisdom, ordains for the redeemed.

The social principles of Christianity preach cowardice, self-contempt, abasement, submissiveness and humbleness, in short, all the qualities of the rabble, and the proletariat, which will not permit itself to be treated as rabble, needs its courage, its self-

confidence, its pride and its sense of independence even more
than its bread.

The social principles of Christianity are sneaking and
hypocritical, and the proletariat is revolutionary.

So much for the social principles of Christianity.[7]

The task for revolutionaries was to free workers from a 'servile
Christian nature', a 'state of religious self-abasement'.[8] This meant
remorseless opposition to Christian Socialism, which Marx loathed
for being half-hearted and tokenistic, more about salving
consciences than taking action. It was merely 'the holy water with
which the priest consecrates the heart-burnings of the aristocrat'.[9]

As well as peddling mental opium, the Established Church was
a mighty land-owner and a hypocrite. It 'is essentially an aristocratic
institution, which must either stand or fall with the landed
oligarchy'.[10] By contrast the more entrepreneurial business class
tended to be Dissenters and resented 'the £13,000,000 annually
abstracted from their pockets by the State Church in England and
Wales alone'.[11] Greed and hypocrisy were rife on both sides. The
Established Church 'will more readily pardon an attack on thirty-
eight of its thirty-nine articles than on one thirty-ninth of its
income';[12] and non-conformist mill-owners kept children working
30 hours at a stretch in the dust-filled 'shoddy-hole'.

> The accused gentlemen affirmed in lieu of taking an oath – as
> Quakers they were too scrupulously religious to take an oath –
> that they had, in their great compassion for the unhappy
> children, allowed them four hours for sleep, but the obstinate
> children absolutely would not go to bed. The Quaker gentlemen
> were fined £20.[13]

Marx was not just objecting to pervasive hypocrisy. Following
Feuerbach, he thought that religion itself involved a basic perceptual
error. In its 'misty realm', 'the products of the human brain appear
as autonomous figures endowed with a life of their own, which enter
into relations both with each other and with the human race'.[14]
The 'supernatural' is merely a projection or distortion of natural,
human powers. In this he was developing, or perhaps vulgarising,
Feuerbach, who had argued on similar lines, whilst retaining a belief
that 'God is an inward spiritual being'.[15]

The antidote to religion was not repression, but reason.
'Everyone should be able to attend to his religious as well as his
bodily needs without the police sticking their noses in.' On the other
hand, a workers' party should endeavour 'to liberate the conscience
from the witchery of religion'.[16] Violent measures against religion
are 'nonsense'.

... as Socialism grows, RELIGION WILL DISAPPEAR. Its disappearance must be done by social development, in which education must play a great part.[17]

Assessment

Marx's scattered writings on religion are significant both for the trenchant critique they make of established theology; and for what they tell us about the development of his own philosophy. He wants to tease out the contradictions in a subject and show how they arise from actual conditions. Having done this, as he thought, with religion, he applied the approach to other subjects.

> True criticism ... shows the inner genesis of the Holy Trinity in the human brain. It describes the act of its birth. So the truly philosophical criticism of the present state constitution not only shows up contradictions as existing: it *explains* them, it comprehends their genesis, their necessity. It considers them in their *specific* significance.[18]

Marx's critique of the 'terrorism of faith'[19] was simple, powerfully and devastatingly simple, but also simplistic. He does not adequately distinguish between religion as a whole and mid-nineteenth-century Christianity in particular, with its mixture of naive literalism, gross hypocrisy and learned obscurantism, the very antithesis of the original teachings of, say, the Sermon on the Mount. He was too quick to announce the death of religion, to declare that, for the masses, religious notions 'have now long been dissolved by circumstance'.[20] He is insufficiently aware of other religious traditions, esoteric, contemplative and mystical; and he underestimates the human propensity to worship something, anything, an idol, a state, or a founding father of socialism. He stated his 'aversion to the personality cult'[21] – as Lenin later did too – but they both overlook the danger that a personality cult, or a form of doctrinaire socialism would become a substitute, cheap and nasty, poor man's religion.

The chief defect of all previous materialism, Marx once noted, was 'that things, reality, sensuousness are conceived only in the form of the object, or of contemplation, but not as sensuous human activity, practice, not subjectively'.[22] This pinpoints the weakness of his own critique of religion. He looks at it only in the form of an object, or even an idea, not 'as sensuous human activity', not in its own right, as specific 'material practice'. Perhaps for this reason, he underestimates its ability to renew itself. He could have considered religion as language, a very potent language to organise beliefs, to inspire, uplift, challenge and empower. Had he done so, he might have been forced into considering the resemblances

between his own beliefs and religious ones. For what Marx shares
with the great religious leaders is an emphasis not just on beliefs,
but on practising and realising them.

Marx's critique of religion was not the coup de grâce he hoped
it might be. Religion flourishes and is all too compatible with an
ability to understand and use advanced technology. Moreover, in
a world where the natural turns out to be even more extraordinary
than previous notions of the supernatural, where scientific fact is
often more wondrous than scriptural fiction, there are opportunities
for new spirituality no longer based on traditional ideas of the
supernatural.

Questions

1. How convincing is Marx's critique of religion?
2. Was Marx right to think that there is something *essentially*
   'reactionary' about religion?
3. Was Marxism itself a religion?

CHAPTER 16

How (not) to Change the World

The philosophers have only interpreted the world in various ways; the point however is to change it.[1]

Did Marx succeed in changing the world? If so, was it for better or worse? What could we learn from his mistakes? What in Marx is dead and what is alive? These are naive questions, but crucial ones, given Marx's absolute commitment to transformation.

Out of Date

Except in a few corners of the world, the arrogant pretensions of 'scientific socialism' are discredited. Marx's theory of class is flawed and so too are his expectations of revolution. His poisonous polemics against opponents are rightly forgotten. More importantly, the two main discourses in which he was writing – that is, Hegelianism and classical economics – are now defunct. Both had been superseded even within his own lifetime.

To see how far we have come from Marx's world, consider his writings about the 'revolution' in 'new means of communication':

On land the Macadamised road has been replaced by the railway, while at sea the slow and irregular sailing ship has been driven into the background by the rapid and regular steamer line; the whole earth has been girded by telegraph cables. It was the Suez canal that really opened the Far East and Australia to the steamer. The circulation time for a shipment of goods to the Far East, which in 1847 was at least twelve months has now been more or less reduced to as many weeks.[2]

Enthusiasm for railways, steamers and telegraph cables seems quaint now we have the 'superhighway'. But emphasis on the importance and impact of the means of communications is obviously still relevant and timely.

Up to Date

One of Marx's abiding insights is the role of technology in shaping society; and the power of those who control technology. Nearly 150 years ago, he was writing about the significance of 'constant revolutionising of production, uninterrupted disturbance of all social conditions, everlasting uncertainty and agitation'; the 'cosmopolitan character to production and consumption in every country'; 'the world market'; and the role of 'immensely facilitated means of communication'.[3] He was one of the first to consider the importance of all this and the far-reaching social consequences of new technology.

Marx's work in this area is strikingly prescient in the age of multinational corporations, and ever-accelerating technological innovation, with revolutionary new means of communication – an increasing range of on-line services, electronic banking, buying and selling of goods over the Internet, interactive TV, cable and video servers, CD-ROMs, multi-media education and entertainment. If we think of Microsoft, the software giant, establishing a strong position across a huge range of service industries, notably banking, telecommunications, publishing and entertainment, then the world of Marx seems a hundred years away, but his analysis – of power and monopoly – remains impressively up to date.

His understanding of the human impact of new technology and his thoughts on alienation will remain relevant wherever dissatisfaction continues, notwithstanding rises in the standard of living. His thoughts on ideology and false consciousness live on in an age of advertising, misinformation and trivialisation. Although communism, in the sense of Soviet style 'command economies', is finished, anyone who wonders whether society can be organised around something other than the profit motive will never wholly get away from the aspirations of Marx and the ideas he pioneered. In these respects, we have not transcended Marx: we have inherited the questions he addressed.

Formative Contradictions

Marx's own method was to unravel the 'contradictions', antagonisms or tensions within a subject; and this invites us to do the same for his own work. His ideas about alienation and false consciousness tend to explain why people are stuck in oppressive conditions and shy away from transforming society. They run counter to his optimism about the inevitability of revolution. Likewise, his insight into the role of technology suggests that power would devolve not to the rank and file proletariat ('brawn workers') but to those who control and develop technology ('brain workers'). It potentially contradicts his confidence in proletarian power.

The most obvious contradiction to explore in Marx's case is between what he wrote and what actually happened in his name. Many of his shortcomings have been exposed by history and by those – including liberals, libertarians, feminists and ecologists – who have criticised his work. These flaws offer an object lesson in how *not* to change the world. They divide into two overlapping groups: a false absolutism and a flawed humanism.

Error upon Error

Marx aimed to discover the 'laws of motion' of capitalist society, rather as Newton had discovered physical laws of motion, or as Darwin had explained evolution. Many of Marx's followers believed that he *had succeeded* in creating a single, all-embracing explanatory system. The tendency to set Marx's ideas in stone, to ossify and calcify them, can be traced back to Engels and the way in which he popularised Marx (especially in *Anti-Dühring*). It was continued by his successors: Kautsky and Plekhanov. Plekhanov in particular tidied Marx's disparate, heterogeneous ideas on philosophy into a unified system he called 'dialectical materialism'. This greatly influenced Lenin. And so it went on. The sceptical, dissident, oppositional potential of Marx's thinking was neglected, in favour of a new orthodoxy. Thus Marx the law-giver triumphed over Marx the creative, flexible thinker.

The belief that Marx's writing was the truth, the whole truth and nothing but the truth could be called the 'monist impulse'. It has important practical consequences, being both a central attraction and a fatal weakness. If everything is to be encompassed in one model, either that model becomes impossibly strained, or contradictory evidence has to be denied and dismissed. On an individual level, absolute faith in one theory can all too easily encourage closedness, defensiveness and conformism; arrogance, authoritarianism, self-importance and fanaticism. It fosters a tendency to control, criticise, organise and police, which itself creates resistance and resentment. Since other groups are by definition in need of guidance, Marxists typically related to them in bad faith, seeking to co-opt and appropriate, creating ill-feeling and new forms of oppression enacted by Marxists themselves.

The monist impulse discourages the kind of diversity and pluralism which allow a system to adapt and evolve. In the case of Marxism, it results organisationally in a rigid hierarchy (with a dire proliferation of committees); economically, in a centralised, command economy, a single planning mechanism and a form of strict state control which suppresses free enterprise; and ideologically, in images of polarisation and perpetual struggle.

Although Marx's outlook was internationalist and cosmopolitan, many of his assumptions remained Eurocentric. The certainty that capitalism had reached its limits and that, like a tottering edifice, it must collapse, was easily felt in crowded, cramped, Victorian London. Had Marx lived in America, or even other parts of Britain, he might have realised how much more room capitalism had to develop.[4] In so far as he prized intellect above wisdom, Marx's rationalism is of a restrictive, Eurocentric kind which virtually ignores the wisdom traditions of its own and other cultures as 'unscientific'. Marx had the limitations of an urban intellectual, a creature of libraries, who had very little time for Nature and who scorned 'the idiocy of rural life'.[5]

Power corrupts. Marx did not specify what kind of power structures to set up after the revolution, to facilitate communication, participation and empowerment, to keep the revolutionary flame burning. He did, however, suggest that all in power should be elected; paid no more than the average worker's wage; and subject to immediate recall (if they start to become corrupt).[6] These are radical, democratic ideas which have never been put into practice.

Marx habitually overlooks the power and significance of small-scale interactions, in the family or in organisations (especially socialist ones). He writes almost nothing about how to improve individual relationships with others, or how to help in an immediate, practical way. All this is displaced on to some notional, future revolution. Marxists do not learn how to sort themselves out in the here-and-now and be happy, independent of the revolution.

Marx has a naive faith in theory as a means to change. He reified (made too much of a thing out of) the critical faculty and over-developed it to the exclusion of other human abilities. He ignored how theory is used for other ends: for status, as a conversation piece; as a conceptual security system; as a bulwark of psychic stasis. He ignores actual human behaviour, applied psychology. He overlooks personal agendas, politics as ego trip.

Looking Forward

In the way it developed, Marxism no longer works as a tool for social change. But that does not nullify the intensity of Marx's commitment to change. He stood, in good part, for an end to complacency and resignation, for a world which has transcended small-mindedness, where global, 'world-historical' responsibility is taken for granted. Because Marx wrote in the possibility of a world transformed, he was more than a merely academic thinker. He could be bold and unreasonable, as in the *Communist Manifesto*, where he spoke as if he had armies up his sleeve, though his followers then numbered a handful. His intellectual style – the scale and scope of the areas he covered – can still inspire anyone oppressed by narrow specialisms. He knew that words can be powerful creative acts which suggest new horizons and open domains of possibility. The tigers of wrath are wiser than the horses of instruction.

In some respects, Marx's critique of capitalism, the profit motive and the 'icy waters of egotistical calculation' – his critique of the world we assume – has never been surpassed. It is perhaps because the world needs change, more than ever, that his mistakes call for ruthless and constructive analysis.

Whether Marx's lifetime work will contribute anything positive to future change largely depends on how it is approached. Marx is best read not as a repository of truth, nor yet as an incarnation of evil, but in a flexible, creative way, at once careful, thorough and free-wheeling, as a lesson in how *not* to change the world, but also as a source of inspiration and ideas.

Questions

1. What aspects of Marx's theory are most impressive and why?
2. How could Marx, whose ideas have obvious limits, have such a huge impact for so long?
3. 'The philosophers have only interpreted the world, in various ways; the point, however, is to change it' (Marx's eleventh Thesis on Feuerbach). Comment.
4. Is it possible to combine the best of socialism with the best of capitalism? If so, how? If not, why not?
5. 'We must emancipate ourselves before we can emancipate others.'[7] What does this mean and how would it relate to Marxism?
6. 'The oppressed either organise against their oppressors or turn on themselves.' Discuss.
7. 'Politics is mostly ego trip.' Justify or refute.
8. The extract below exemplifies a philosophy of 'abundant life'.

   The truth about this earth is that it is an infinitely good, beautiful, nourishing place to be. The only 'evil' comes from lack of understanding of this truth. Evil (ignorance) is like a shadow – it has no real substance of its own, it is simply a lack of light. You cannot cause a shadow to disappear by trying to fight it, stamp on it, by railing against it, or any other form of emotional or physical resistance. In order to cause a shadow to disappear, you must shine light on it.[8]

   Set out how you think Marx would have responded.

9. 'Marx never looks at in-betweens, but only at extremes.' Discuss.

Afterword

In summarising Marx, something is altered and something lost. A synopsis edits out his digressions, his inconsistencies, his moments of suggestive disorder. In filtering out the more subjective – emotional, moral, imaginative, poetic, mythic – aspects of his prose, we lose both its characteristic texture and its formative contradictions. And with these we lose textual evidence about his character (the folly and the genius) and the fateful defects which were passed on and amplified in the culture of Marxism. All this is the subject for another book.

Appendix 1 The Attraction of Marxism

What was the attraction of Marxism? Or, to put the question more starkly: why, given evidence of, for example, Stalin's purges, did Marxism continue to have a hold on many in the West?

I begin with some of the 'positive' reasons why people might believe in Marxism; and then speculate about more negative pay-offs.

1. *An alternative to capitalism/imperialism.* Many people blamed capitalism for urbanisation, mass poverty, recession, colonialism and war. Marxism promised an end to all this – an end to inequality, competition, selfishness, exploitation and greed.
2. *The historical record.* Up to 1917 Marxism had not been tried out. In the 1920s, people blamed capitalism for the atrocities of the First World War; and in the 1930s for recession. Compared with Marxists, other groups seemed weak and irresolute before Nazism. And when war came, 'it was the Red Army that ripped the guts out of the filthy Nazis', as Churchill put it.
3. *Vision of equality and justice:* fairer distribution of wealth; a society of equals, free from poverty, which values everyone; the people (through the state) owning the means of production; production for social needs before profit; political solidarity and camaraderie; a classless, rational, emancipating society. *Communism* promised an abundance of goods; an end to the age-long problems of homelessness and hunger; an end to the envy and anger of the oppressed and to the fear and guilt of the oppressor; the eventual 'withering away of the state', along with its means of coercion (the police and the law courts).
4. Related to the above, a vision of 'universally developed individuals';[1] an end to the division of labour and to alienation. Communism, according to Marx, is 'the only society in which the original and free development of individuals ceases to be a mere phrase'.[2] He shared the aspiration of the Utopian socialists that 'anyone in whom there is a potential Raphael should be able to develop without hindrance';[3] 'the free development of each is a condition for the free development of all'.[4] Socialism envisages an end to society organised around competition and inequality. It suggests that greed is a *learned* behaviour. It is

143

based on an *optimistic view of human potential*. Marx created a
core, or critical mass, of ideals, to which other people could bring
their own.

5. Marxism presented a way to *understand the world and change it*.
   It could supply a sense of empowerment; having the key to
   history; being right; able to prove others wrong.[5] The system
   was neat and its claim to be all-embracing offered a kind of
   artistic satisfaction. Intellectuals could enjoy the claims of
   Marxism to realism and totality; delight in some simple answers
   to complex problems; relish their privileged understanding of
   his complexities; and marvel at the bold, lofty scale of his vision.

6. *Pride*. If Marxism contained the secret of history, it offered a
   sense of revelation, as if its followers were the enlightened few,
   an elite corps to guide the benighted masses. Nothing could be
   more calculated to flatter the vanities and susceptibilities of the
   intelligentsia.

7. *Other psychological pay-offs*. A sense of security to head off,
   explain away or control encounters with the unknown; a way
   of expressing anger, resentment or general anti-authoritarian-
   ism (against, for example, capitalism or the state); subconscious
   identification with Marx (as, for example, displaced intellectual,
   lone genius, defiant rebel, authority figure or intellectual
   frontiersman). For the intelligentsia, Marxism could be a chic
   fashion, a way of posing as a rebel, but also indulging in a kind
   of conformism, or even careerism.

8. *Social pay-offs*. A way to classify people; label them as types (for
   example, 'petty bourgeois' or 'lumpen'); meet the like-minded
   on known ground, safe within a conceptual framework; despise
   and avoid others. A way of belonging, to a secret club and/or a
   mass movement.

9. A more or less submerged *romanticism* which offered potentially
   heroic scripts: being a champion of the oppressed; an
   underground leader; an agent of History; a doomed hero. Marx
   storms heaven in the name of empowering humans. Marxism
   may be seen as an act of defiance against the tyranny of poverty
   and greed; as a male power trip; or as fodder for the imagination
   and for legitimate human aspirations.

These various factors contributed to Marxism as a quasi-religious
revelation, able to inspire faith, devotion, passion and zeal.

Appendix 2 Violence, Negativity and Failure

Why is Marx connected with violence, conflict and negativity?

It could be simply that the world changed in ways Marx neither predicted nor understood. Knowing at some level they were wrong, but unable to admit their failure, later Marxists sank into confusion and viciousness.

The explanations below suggest that it was more than merely a false anticipation. Marx's approach was intrinsically flawed. The seeds of negativity were buried deep within it. Marxism was therefore doomed to failure and had to resort to terror to prop itself up.

1. Imbalance ↗ Maslow

All humans need to fulfil themselves at the physical, emotional, mental and spiritual levels. Marx was too focused on the mental dimension. His expectations of theory were unrealistically high. This encouraged the neglect or repression of other levels, which leads to unhappiness and aggression. Marxism was unhealthy because it was unbalanced. Its history is a cautionary tale for all intellectuals.

2. Human Nature

Marx's focus on reason led to a complete misjudgement about human behaviour as a whole. Socialism could not work because of basic human propensities: people's natural self-seeking, greed and need for incentives (such as profit). Marx's idea that all this could change under socialism was hopelessly hopeful. Capitalism at least allows for human selfishness – and flourishes on it – instead of expecting us to become otherwise. It is easier to move an ocean than to change one drop of human nature.

3. Latent Authoritarianism

If human beings have deep instincts to lead or to be led, it may be that they are not fitted for equality, that equality could only be *imposed* on them. This leads to repression and resentment, perhaps to a police state. At the economic level, the absence of the market leads to domination by central government, bureaucracy and political authoritarianism.

4. Anti-religion

Marx had good reason to condemn the churches of his time for their hypocrisy. But he mistakenly threw out the 'baby' of spirituality along with the dirty 'bath-water' of institutionalised religion. In theory, Marxism was to put an end to control and interference by religious institutions; and leave spiritual matters to the individual. In practice, its deep hostility to religion could stop its followers from developing their spiritual resources and their capacity for goodness.

5. Anti-morality

Marx was unclear about the role of morality. Sometimes he seemed to suggest that all morality was merely 'false consciousness' or 'bourgeois prejudice'. He also implied that the ends could justify the means, without providing any clear moral stopping point. So his followers were ethically disabled or even disarmed, which encouraged the rise of thugs like Stalin.

6. No Psychology

Marx's early work about alienation contains a good deal of understanding (for its time) about social psychology. This was all but lost as he went on to write about political economy. The later writing has very little about psychology and Marxists were often ignorant and inept in this area.

7. Negative Emotions

Marx's mind was contaminated by frustration, anger and hatred. In the long run, such emotions are destructive. Communist groups were infiltrated by police spies which bred suspicion, fear and hostility. Marxists tried to set up hate figures and enemy images to stoke radical anger with the aim of converting it into action. Anger gives a quick kick, but is no basis for a long-term campaign.

8. Intellectual Aggression

'Criticism,' Marx wrote, 'is not a lancet, it is a weapon. Its object is its *enemy*, which it wants not to refute but to *exterminate*.'[1] He thought that ideas developed through conflict and argument. His favourite genres, critique and polemic, are symptoms of intellectual aggression and sow the seeds for actual violence. They select, distort and exaggerate, increasing areas of disagreement. Marx too often dismissed the merits of others' views or the spirit in which they were offered. It is better to adopt a softer, more conciliatory, 'holistic' approach.

9. Anti-utopianism

Marx wanted to distinguish his work from the likes of Fourier and Robert Owen, 'Utopians' who dreamed up grand, imaginary schemes for the future. He scorned 'the play of the imagination on the future structure of society'.[2] By disparaging visionaries, he discouraged the education of desire and the free play of imagination, which are vital for the future development of socialism.

10. False Scientism

In contrast to the 'Utopian socialists', Marx wanted to focus on understanding the present. He called this brand of socialism 'scientific' and wrote in the manner of a scientist, uncovering social laws, as Darwin had discovered natural ones.[3] To put it strongly, Marx was often dressing up his own wishes and commitments in scientific language, the dominant discourse of the time.

I have been making general remarks about Marx as a whole. His followers, if they acknowledge that there is anything flawed in his approach, tend to focus on details. Perhaps some aspect of his economic theory needs fine-tuning; perhaps there are some loose threads in the transformation problem; perhaps his work needs supplementing with a new awareness of ethnicity and gender. Whatever, in their view, the essence of Marx is correct. One way of maintaining this is to allow that there are errors, but to focus on what went wrong *after* his death.

1. Engels

In the years around Marx's death, Engels turned Marx's open, creative and exploratory approach into a systematic dogma. He amplified and reinforced Marx's own predilection for 'scientific laws'. Marxism started to become the very kind of doctrinaire religion which Marx himself had deplored.[4]

2. Plekhanov and Kautsky

The tendency to systematise Marx was deepened by Plekhanov and Kautsky, the leading Marxists in the years after Engels' death. In

1891 Plekhanov had first characterised Marx's philosophy as 'dialectical materialism'. This implied that Marx had discovered an infallible method which just needed to be applied and the correct answer would pop up, like bread out of a toaster. This became a caricature of Marx's actual practice. A sceptical, flexible, broad-ranging way of thinking was re-hashed as a ghastly pseudo-science: a mix of positivism, dogmatism and mysticism. At the political level, Plekhanov spoke of the 'dictatorship of the proletariat', not in Marx's sense of 'the proletariat organised as the ruling class',[5] but as an enlightened vanguard, who must organise and control working people.

3. Lenin

Marxism was further deformed by Lenin, who had not seen Marx's early, humanistic writings. Lenin laid the seeds for totalitarianism and repression by insisting on strict party discipline and 'democratic centralism' – a contradiction in terms. (This view was often taken by anarchists and 'left wing communists', such as Pannekoek.) Lenin's devastating polemics often abused original or divergent thinkers, accusing them of 'eclecticism'.

4. Lack of Democracy

Because Marxist states had no sound procedure for changing their leaders, the dictatorships grew increasingly old, complacent and ineffective. The seeds of this problem were sown early and grew into the rotten fruits of Brezhnev's gerontocracy and the 'era of stagnation', before the collapse of state socialism.

5. Stalin

Marxism was doing well until the late 1920s when Stalin tragically hijacked the Communist Party, murdered the leading Bolsheviks and liquidated the richer peasants ('kulaks') in the Great Purges of the 1930s. Stalin advocated 'socialism in one country', although Marx had stated 'communism is only possible as the act of the dominant peoples "all at once" and simultaneously'.[6]

6. Imperialism

Those who fight dragons themselves become dragons.

Marxism was not violent itself; violence was inflicted on it by its enemies. The new workers' state in Russia was attacked by imperialist armies. Winston Churchill gave orders to 'strangle communism in its cradle'.[7] Western leaders encouraged the Nazis to prepare invasion of the Soviet Union. Under attack from all fronts, the USSR fell into a damaging 'siege mentality' and an economically crippling militarism.

6. Khruschev

Marxism was working until the early 1950s when Khrushchev led a new bourgeoisie to power in the USSR. (This classic, Stalinist, or Marxist-Leninist view, is no longer much heard.)

7. A 'Die-hard' View

Marxism was working until the late 1980s when Gorbachev capitulated to militarist pressure from the USA. Even so, the backward, semi-feudal, 'Third World' country of 1917, had become a modern nation, with an impressive welfare state.

8. Another View

Real Marxism has never been tried, so we cannot say that it has 'gone bad'. Marx and Lenin called for election of workers as representatives, but also recall at any time; their pay not to exceed that of a worker; devolution of power; and control and supervision by all.[8] None of this happened in the USSR, which was a dictatorship or bureaucracy, not a true workers' state. The main problem with Marxism is that no one has tried it.

Questions

1. Some of the above views are mutually exclusive, but most are not. How would you combine them (perhaps with other theories) to give a full explanation for the violent, negative aspects of Marxism?
2. Which of the above explanations for the connection between Marxism and violence do you find *least* convincing?
3. Is Marx responsible for the evils of Marxism? Is Christ responsible for the horrific deeds of the Church? Is any leader responsible for what their followers do with their work?

Notes and References

References throughout are to *The Collected Works of Karl Marx and Frederick Engels*, published by Lawrence and Wishart, London, in association with Progress Publishers, Moscow. In the footnotes, I abbreviate this to *CW*, followed by the volume and page number. Thus *CW*, 47, 90 refers to the *Collected Works*, volume 47, page 90. Sometimes references are run together. Thus CW, 47, 90, 120, 125 refers to those three pages of volume 47. Occasionally, where they are considerably better, I use other translations, showing the source and also, where possible, giving a reference to the corresponding passage in the *Collected Works*. I use the Penguin edition of *Capital*.

For letters, I save space by using the standard English conventions. Thus Marx, 1/5/64 would refer to a letter written by Marx on 1 May 1864. Marx wrote mostly in German. Where he uses an English phrase, this is shown in the text by CAPITAL LETTERS.

It is a strange fact that, well over a hundred years after Marx's death, the publication of his *Collected Works* is still not complete.

A Private Life

1. Engels to Marx, 10/3/53, *CW*, 38, 335; 39, 283.
2. Jenny Marx, 'Short Sketch of an Eventful Life', in Payne, Robert, ed., *The Unknown Karl Marx*, University of London Press, London, 1972, p. 126.
3. Jenny Marx to Louise Weydemeyer, 11/3/61, *CW*, 41, 570.
4. *CW*, 40, 328–31.
5. *CW*, 40, 374.
6. *CW*, 40, 432; 41, 216, 292.
7. *CW*, 40, 217, 224, 249.
8. *CW*, 41, 574.
9. Marx to Kugelmann, 28/12/62, *CW*, 41, 436.
10. *CW*, 45, 37, 278.
11. Marx to Engels, *CW*, 39, 181–2.
12. Engels to Bernstein, 2–3/11/82, *CW*, 46, 356. Also Engels to C. Schmidt, 5/8/90, in *Marx and Engels Selected Works, in One Volume*, [hereinafter *SW*] Lawrence and Wishart, London, 1968, p. 689.
13. Paul Lafargue (Marx's son-in-law), 'Reminiscences of Marx', First pub. 1890, in *Marx and Engels Through the Eyes of their Contemporaries*, [hereinafter, *Eyes*], Progress Publishers, Moscow, 1978, p. 29.
14. Ibid.
15. Ibid, 30.
16. Ibid, 41.

17. Marx to his daughter Laura, 11/4/68, *CW*, 43, 10.
18. Liebknecht, in *Eyes*, p. 70.
19. Marx to Jenny Longuet, 7/12/81, *CW*, 46, 156.
20. Franziska Kugelmann, 'Small Traits of Marx's Great Character', First pub. 1928, in *Eyes*, p. 233.
21. Friedrich Lessner, 'Before 1848 and After: Reminiscences of an Old Communist', First pub. 1898, in *Eyes*, p.130.
22. Liebknecht, in *Eyes*, p. 102.
23. Report by police spy to the Prussian authorities. Cited in Shwarzschild, *The Red Prussian*, p. 219.
24. *CW*, 42, 567–9. I have amalgamated two different versions.
25. Kugelmann, in *Eyes*, p. 238.
26. Lafargue, in *Eyes*, p. 33.
27. Ibid., 31.

Unhappiness and Alienation

1. T.S. Eliot, *The Waste Land*, Faber and Faber, London, 1922.
2. See chapter on 'Class and Society'. Also Marx's discussion of alienation in the 'Resultate', written in the mid-1860s, but not published until 1933; in *Capital*, I, 1003.
3. *Capital*, I, 899.
4. Marx, *Economic and Philosophic Manuscripts of 1844* [hereinafter, *EPM*], *CW*, 3, 279.
5. Ibid., p. 274.
6. Ibid., p. 272.
7. *EPM*, *CW*, 3, 274.
8. Marx, 'Comments on James Mill', 1844, *CW*, 3, 227–8.
9. *Wage Labour and Capital*, *CW*, 9, 202–3.
10. Linton Kwesi Johnson,*Tings & Times*, Selected Poems, Bloodaxe Books, Newcastle upon Tyne 1991, pp. 13–14.
11. *EPM*, *CW*, 3, p. 273.
12. Ibid., 272.
13. Ibid., 271–2.
14. *The German Ideology*, *CW*, 5, 47.
15. *Manifesto of the Communist Party*, *CW*, 6, 490–1. Nowadays there may also be a devaluation of skills, with skilled workers (for example, machinists) treated and paid as unskilled workers.
16. *EPM*, *CW*, 3, 277.
17. *The Holy Family*, *CW*, 4, 36. Marx makes the same point, less concisely, in his 'Economic Manuscript of 1861-3', *CW*, 34, 398–9.
18. Geshe Kelsang Gyatso, *A Meditation Handbook*, Tharpa Publications, London, 1990, pp. 3–4.
19. *The German Ideology*, *CW*, 5, 51.
20. *Manifesto of the Communist Party*, *CW*, 6, 511.
21. Marx, 'Speech at the Anniversary of the People's Paper', 1856. Marx and Engels, *Selected Works*, I, pp. 359–60. Cf. *Capital*, I, 798–9, where Marx says that new technologies 'alienate from [the worker] the intellectual potentialities of the labour process'.
22. *Capital*, I, 547.

23. *Grundrisse, CW*, 28, 465. See also *CW*, 28, 389–90 and the section marked 'alienation' in *CW*, 29, 209–11.
24. 'Economic Manuscript of 1861–3', *CW*, 34, 526. Index.
25. 'Economic Manuscript of 1861–3', *CW*, 34, 200–2.
26. Ibid., 243–5.
27. Ibid., 246.
28. 'Economic Manuscript of 1861–3', *CW*, 33, 491.
29. Marx, 'Provisional Rules of the Association' [First International], *CW*, 20, 14.
30. Ann Oakley, *Housewife*, Allen Lane, London, 1974.
31. Frantz Fanon, *Black Skin, White Masks*, MacGibbon and Kee, London, 1968 (First pub. 1952).

How Marx (re)wrote History

1. *Capital*, I, 897–8.
2. *Capital*, I, translation by Samuel Moore and Edward Aveling. *CW*, 35, 739.
3. Hegel, *The Philosophy of History* (trans. Sibree), Dover Publications, New York, 1956, pp. 410–11. This is the start of the final paragraph of his chapter on 'the transition from feudalism to monarchy', which also concludes his section on 'the German world'.
4. . *Capital*, I, 851–3.

History According to Marx

1. 'Overthrown by the ruling elite?' Fred Weir, *Morning Star*, 26 May 1994, p. 5. The study was prepared by Olga Krishtanovskaya and its conclusions reported in *Izvestia*.
2. *Capital*, I, 273.
3. *Manifesto of the Communist Party, CW*, 6, 489.
4. Ibid., 485–6.
5. Ibid., 487–90.
6. *Capital*, I, 876.
7. Ibid., 874.
8. Ibid., 879.
9. Ibid.
10. *Grundrisse, CW*, 28, 464.
11. *Capital*, I, 881–3.
12. Ibid., 878.
13. Ibid., 906–7.
14. Ibid., 875.
15. Ibid., 895.
16. Alan Carling, 'Analytical Marxism and Historical Materialism: the Debate on Social Evolution', *Science and Society*, Vol. 57, No. 1, Spring 1993, pp. 31–65.
17. Marx, Preface to *A Contribution to the Critique of Political Economy*, 1859, *CW*, 29, 263.
18. In social theory, words like 'definite', 'certain' and 'determinate' usually mean 'indefinite', 'uncertain' and 'indeterminate'.

19. This is called the Development Thesis. The idea that the level of development of the productive forces explains the nature of the production relations is called the Primacy Thesis. Here I am following in the wake of G.A. Cohen.

20. *Capital*, I, 916. Marx uses the German word *Gewalt*, meaning force or violence. C.f. Engels to Conrad Schmidt, 27/10/90: 'Force, that is state power, is also an economic power!', *SW*, 689.

21. In the French translation, Marx softened 'bedingt' into 'domine en général'.

22. Preface to *A Contribution to the Critique of Political Economy*, *CW*, 29, 263.

23. *Grundrisse*, *CW*, 28, 46. Marx's italics. To smudge matters further, the 'mode of co-operation, or social stage' is also a productive force. (*German Ideology*, *CW*, 5, 43); and 'the greatest productive power is the revolutionary class itself' (*Poverty of Philosophy*, *CW*, 6, 211). Moreover, 'society's general science, KNOWLEDGE, has become an *immediate productive force*' (*Grundrisse*, *CW*, 29, 92); mechanisation can allow an 'increase of free time, i.e. time for the full development of the individual, which itself, as the greatest productive force, in turn reacts upon the productive power of labour' (*Grundrisse*, *CW*, 29, 97).

24. 'Reflections of a Young Man on the Choice of a Profession', essay written by Marx aged 17, *CW*, 1, 4.

25. *Capital*, I, 91. Preface to the first edition.

26. *The German Ideology*, *CW*, 5, 438.

27. *The Poverty of Philosophy*, *CW*, 6, 170.

28. *The German Ideology*, *CW*, 5, 54.

29. *The Eighteenth Brumaire of Louis Bonaparte*, *CW*, 11, 103.

30. *Capital*, III, Lawrence and Wishart, London, 1974, Chapter 47, p. 791. Italics added. See also *Capital*, III, Penguin, 1981, p. 927.

31. *The Holy Family*, *CW*, 4, 37.

32. Ibid., 93.

33. *Manifesto of the Communist Party*, *CW*, 6, 483.

34. See Jon Elster, *Making Sense of Marx*, Cambridge University Press, Cambridge, 1985. To follow his argument and his examples, read the pages referred to under 'functional explanation' in his index.

35. Marx, letter to a Russian magazine, 1877, *CW*, 24, 200–1.

36. Engels to Conrad Schmidt, 5/8/90, *SW*, 679.

37. Criticisms of a paradigm generate new historical approaches. Thus the Whig interpretation of history (unilinear political Progress) gave way to the Marxist; the Marxist to the revisionist; and the revisionist perhaps to a new kind of history, not yet named, but which might be called 'total history', which repudiates Marx's belief in Revolution and his notion of class, but is heavily influenced by his stress on *the people* as a whole, not leading personalities.

Class and Society

1. 'Persona Behaviourgraphics Classification', 1994, by CCN Systems Ltd.

2. Apart from these, there is also an 'Asiatic mode of production', such as the former Chinese empire, where a class of imperial officers and

priests live off the work of the majority. This mode of production is internally stable, or stagnant.

3. *Wage Labour and Capital*, *CW*, 9, 203.
4. *Manifesto of the Communist Party*, *CW*, 6, 494.
5. *Capital*, III, 1025–6 (that is, the final chapter).
6. 'Theories of Surplus Value. Ricardo', 'Economic Manuscript of 1861–3', *CW*, 32, 198.
7. *Capital*, III, 735–6.
8. Marx, 'Moralizing Criticism and Critical Morality', *CW*, 6, 330.
9. Robin Blackburn was an early researcher into unionisation and white collar workers. Kees van der Pijl attempts an important project in *The Making of an Atlantic Ruling Class*, Verso, London, 1984. There is room for a similar book on the growth of a Pacific ruling class.
10. See Chapter on 'Exploitation and Economics'.
11. A further 'contradiction' could be created by the increasing elderly population – the *greying* of capitalism. New medical technologies greatly extend the post-working life, not contributing to profit, but siphoning it off. This creates a contradiction between, on the one hand, the individual or family will to prolong life span; and on the other hand, the collective needs of capital. The individual is striking back against the species (*EPM*, *CW*, 3, 299). At the end of his life, Marx wrote 'MOST OF MY *CONTEMPORARIES*, I MEAN FELLOWS OF THE SAME AGE, JUST NOW KICK THE BUCKET in gratifying numbers. There are too many young donkeys for the old ones to be kept alive' (*CW*, 46, 398). The growing numbers of elderly donkeys could eat into the profits of capitalist society.
12. *The Class Struggles in France'*, *CW*, 10, 116.
13. Ibid., 48.
14. Ibid., 50.
15. Ibid., 49.
16. Ibid., 117.
17. Ibid., 57.
18. Ibid., 61, 120.
19. Ibid., 74.
20. Ibid., 62.
21. Ibid., 110.
22. Ibid., 81.
23. Marx, 'The Elections in England – Tories and Whigs', 2/8/52, *CW*, 11, 331.
24. Marx to Weydemeyer, 5/3/52, *CW*, 39, 64–5.
25. See chapter on Colonialism.
26. Michael Levin, 'Marx and Engels on the National Question', *Studies in Marxism*, 2, 1995, pp. 113–33.

The Politics of Revolution

1. *Manifesto of the Communist Party*, Part III, *CW*, 6, 507–17. Also *The German Ideology*, *CW*, 5, 453–581.
2. *Capital*, I, Postface to the second edition, p. 99.
3. *The German Ideology*, *CW*, 5, 90.

4. 'The Civil War in France', CW, 22, 329–30. A fuller account of Marx's writing on the State is given in Jon Elster, *Making Sense of Marx*, Cambridge University Press, Cambridge, 1985, pp. 398–428.
5. *The Poverty of Philosophy*, CW, 6, 211.
6. Ibid., 210.
7. 'Value, Price and Profit', (1865), CW, 20, 149. See also CW, 20, 191–2.
8. *Manifesto of the Communist Party*, CW, 6, 498.
9. Ibid., 493.
10. Ibid., 496.
11. Marx and Engels, 'Address to the Communist League', 1850, CW, 10, 281.
12. Ibid., 282–3.
13. Ibid., 285.
14. Ibid., 286–7.
15. 'The Class Struggles in France', CW, 10, 135.
16. 'Revelations Concerning the Communist Trial in Cologne', CW, 11, 403.
17. Marx to Bolte, 23/11/71, CW, 44, 252.
18. 'The Civil War in France', CW, 22, 354.
19. Marx to Kugelmann, 9/10/66, CW, 42, 326.
20. Marx, interview with a correspondent from *The World*, CW, 22, 601.
21. Marx to Engels, 11/9/67, CW, 42, 424.
22. See 'Provisional Rules of the Association', CW, 20, 14.
23. Marx and Engels, 'Circular Letter', 17–18/9/79, CW, 45, 408.
24. 'Sir Mountstuart Elphinstone Grant Duff's account of a talk with Karl Marx', CW, 24, 580–2.
25. Engels to Bernstein, 12–13/6/83, CW, 47, 35.
26. Engels, 'Introduction to K. Marx's *The Class Struggles in France*', CW, 27, 521–2.
27. 'Inaugural Address of the Association', CW, 20, 11–12. Also CW, 20, 190; 22, 335.
28. *Class Struggles in France, 1848–1850*, CW, 10, 122.
29. Marx, interview with the *Chicago Tribune*, 1878, CW, 24, 576.
30. Marx, Speech in Amsterdam, 8/9/72, CW, 23, 255. Cf. Engels' remarks at the end of his Preface to the English edition of *Capital*, 1886.
31. *Capital*, I, Chapter 10. Also 'Instructions for the Delegates at the Geneva Conference, 1866', CW, 20, 187.
32. *The German Ideology*, CW, 5, 75.
33. Marx and Engels, 'Review of Guizot', CW, 10, 254–5.
34. Marx, 'The Chartists', CW, 11, 335.
35. 'Russia Using Austria', *New York Daily Tribune*, 10/10/60, CW, 17, 486. Other examples are given in Elster, *Making Sense of Marx*, pp. 379–90.

Socialism and Communism

1. *The German Ideology*, CW, 5, 49.
2. *Manifesto of the Communist Party*, CW, 6, 498.

3. Ibid., 500.
4. Ibid., 499–503.
5. Ibid., 504.
6. Ibid., 505. In 1872, Marx notes that this passage 'would in many respects be very differently worded today', *CW*, 23, 175.
7. *EPM*, *CW*, 3, 296–7.
8. 'Critique of the Gotha Programme', 1875, *CW*, 24, 85.
9. Ibid., 87.
10. Ibid., 95.
11. Marx uses the phrase 'dictatorship of the proletariat' in *Class Struggles in France, 1848–50*, *CW*, 10, 127; and in a letter to Weydemeyer of 5/3/52. The phrase was probably coined shortly before that by the French revolutionary Blanqui.
12. *Capital*, III, 911.
13. 'The Nationalisation of the Land', *CW*, 23, 131–6.
14. *Capital*, I, 171–2.
15. *The German Ideology*, *CW*, 5, 394.
16. *Capital*, II, 434.
17. *The Civil War in France*, *CW*, 22, 333.
18. Ibid., 334.
19. Marx to Domela-Nieuwenhuis, 22/2/81, *CW*, 46, 66.
20. Marx, 'Inaugural Address of the First International', *CW*, 20, 11.
21. 'Critique of Hegel's *Philosophy of Right* [Recht]', McLellan, David, *Karl Marx: Selected Writings*, Oxford University Press, Oxford, 1977, p. 31. Also *CW*, 3, 46–7.
22. *The Eighteenth Brumaire of Louis Bonaparte*, *CW*, 11, 185.
23. Drafts to 'Civil War in France', *CW*, 22, 534.
24. Marx to Kugelmann, 12/4/71, *CW*, 44, 131. Lenin emphasises this phrase in *The State and Revolution*.
25. Cited in Leopold Schwarzschild, *The Red Prussian: The Life and Legend of Karl Marx*, Hamish Hamilton, London, 1948, p. 80.
26. Engels to Marx, 30/7/69, *CW*, 43, 336.
27. 'Notes on Bakunin's *Statehood and Anarchy*', *CW*, 24, 520.

Ideology

1. *The German Ideology*, *CW*, 5, 36–7.
2. Ibid., 59.
3. *Capital*, I, Postface to the second edition, p. 98.
4. *Capital*, I, 899.
5. *Capital*, I, 175. The political economist is the 'ideologist' of the capitalist. Ibid., 718.
6. *Grundrisse*, *CW*, 28, 389.
7. *Capital*, I, Preface to the French edition, p. 104.
8. Marx, *Introduction to the Critique of Hegel's Philosophy of Recht*, *CW*, 3, 182.
9. *The Holy Family*, *CW*, 4, 119.
10. Preface to the *Economic and Philosophic Manuscripts* of 1844, *CW*, 3, 231.
11. Marx to Meyer and Vogt, 9/4/70, *CW*, 43, 474–5. See also p. 398.

12. 'English Ferocity in China', March 1857, in *On Colonialism*, Lawrence and Wishart, London, 1959, p. 115.
13. Marx, 'Report of the General Council', August 1872, *CW*, 23, 226.
14. Marx, 'Notes on Wagner's *Lehrbuch der politischen Oekonomie*', *CW*, 24, 553.
15. *Grundrisse*, *CW*, 28, 176.
16. Valentin Nikolaevich Volosinov (also known as Mikhail Bakhtin), *Marxism and the Philosophy of Language*, Seminar Press, New York, 1973.
17. 'The Coming Election in England', 31 March 1857, in *On Colonialism*, Lawrence and Wishart, 1976, p. 109.
18. Michael Foucault, *Language, Counter-memory, Practice: Selected Essays and Interviews*, Cornell University Press, Ithaca NY, 1977.
19. Adrian Mitchell, *Collected Poems*, Allison and Busby, London, 1982, p. 65.

Philosophy

1. Marx, 'Leading Article of No. 179 of *Kölnische Zeitung*', *CW*, 1, 195.
2. *The German Ideology*, *CW*, 5, 56.
3. 'Theses on Feuerbach', No. 11, *CW*, 5, 5.
4. In this context, materialism does not mean the accumulation of possessions, nor does idealism mean high-mindedness. Philosophical materialism takes the physical world as the main reality. Sociological materialism holds that people are motivated mainly by material interests.
5. 'The Leading Article of No. 179 of *Kölnische Zeitung*', *CW*, 1, 201.
6. *The Holy Family*, *CW*, 4, 128.
7. *Capital*, I, 494.
8. *The German Ideology*, *CW*, 5, 36.
9. See the section 'Critique of the Hegelian Dialectic and Philosophy as a Whole', at the end of *EPM*, *CW*, 3, 326–46.
10. Preface to *A Contribution to the Critique of Political Economy*, *CW*, 29, 264.
11. *The Poverty of Philosophy*, *CW*, 6, 162–5. See also Mueller, Gustav E., 'The Hegel Legend of "thesis-antithesis-synthesis"', *Journal of the History of Ideas*, June 1958, pp. 411–14.
12. 'Revolution in China and in Europe', 14/6/53, *CW*, 12, 93.
13. Marx to Engels, 16/1/58, *CW*, 40, 249.
14. Marx, Postface to the second edition of *Capital*, Vol. I, pp. 102–3.
15. Ludwig Feuerbach, *The Essence of Christianity* (trans. G. Eliot), Harper and Row, New York, 1957, p. 226.
16. 'Theses on Feuerbach', No. 11, *CW*, 5, 5.
17. Jindric Zeleny, *The Logic of Marx*, Basil Blackwell, Oxford, 1980.
18. Roslyn Wallach Bologh, *Dialectical Phenomenology: Marx's Method*, Routledge and Kegan Paul, London, 1979.
19. *Capital*, I, Preface to first edition, p. 91.
20. *Capital*, I, 798.
21. Ibid., 784.
22. Ibid., 92.

23. See David Walker, 'Marx and Scientific Positivism', *Studies in Marxism*, 2, 1995, pp. 13–36.
24. 'On the Jewish Question', *CW*, 3, 162–8.
25. Ibid., 164.
26. Ibid., 168.
27. *Capital*, I, Postface to the second edition, p. 102.
28. *The German Ideology*, *CW*, 5, 39.
29. Ibid. The example probably alludes to Fourier, who had the bizarre idea that cherries result from the earth copulating with itself.
30. *EPM*, *CW*, 3, 299.
31. Ibid., 298.
32. *The German Ideology*, *CW*, 5, 438.
33. *Capital*, I, 144.
34. *German Ideology*, *CW*, 5, 44. Cf. *Grundrisse*, *CW*, 28, 99. 'Ideas do not exist apart from language.' The implications of this for the philosophy of consciousness were developed by the Russian thinker, Mikhail Bakhtin, also known as Medvedev and Volosinov. See *The Formal Method in Literary Scholarship* and *Marxism and the Philosophy of Language*.
35. *The German Ideology*, *CW*, 5, 36.
36. *Capital*, I, 149.
37. *Grundrisse*, *CW*, 28, 195. See also Ibid., 18; and *Wage Labour and Capital*, *CW*, 9, 211.
38. *Wage Labour and Capital*, *CW*, 9, 216.
39. 'Theses on Feuerbach', No. 8, *CW*, 5, 5.
40. *The German Ideology*, *CW*, 5, 41–2.
41. Ibid., 53–4.
42. Ibid., 54.
43. Ibid., 37. Translation amended in line with David McLellan, *Karl Marx: Selected Writings*, Oxford University Press, Oxford, 1977, p. 165.
44. *The German Ideology*, *CW*, 5, 236.
45. Ibid., p. 262–3.
46. 'On the Jewish Question', *CW*, 3, 169–70.

Exploitation and Economics

1. *Capital*, I, Preface to the first edition, 92.
2. *Value, Price and Profit*, *CW*, 20, 105.
3. Engels, 'Review of Marx's *Contribution to the Critique of Political Economy*', *CW*, 16, 476.
4. *EPM*, *CW*, 3, 270–1.
5. *Capital*, III, 959.
6. Marx to Engels, 2/4/58, *CW*, 40, 298. See also *CW*, 40, 270, 376. And Rosdolsky.
7. Information supplied by Nike, and field research by Christian Aid in Bethan Brookes and Peter Madden, *The Globe-Trotting Sports Shoe*, Christian Aid, London, 1995. The report is on the World Wide Web: http://www.oneworld.org/christian_aid/.

8. See *Capital*, I, Chapter 27, 'The Expropriation of the Agricultural Population from the Land'.
9. Marx, 'Political Indifferentism', *CW*, 23, 393.
10. *Capital*, I, 325.
11. Ibid.
12. Ibid., 672.
13. Ibid., 728.
14. Ibid., 266.
15. *Capital*, III, 957–8.
16. *Value, Price and Profit*, *CW*, 20, 127.
17. Marx describes it in *Capital*, Chapter 10.
18. *Value, Price and Profit*, *CW*, 20, 122.
19. Ibid., 124.
20. Ibid.
21. Ibid., 123–4.
22. Ibid., 118.
23. Ibid., 126.
24. *The Poverty of Philosophy*, *CW*, 6, 126. Marx's answer seems to smuggle supply and demand back into the picture.
25. *Capital*, I, 695.
26. *Capital*, I, 167.
27. My criticism here is similar to Marx's criticism of Hegel (in *Critique of Hegel's 'Philosophy of Right'*) for having started with abstract ideas instead of concrete reality. Marx accused Hegel of focusing on 'the life-process of the idea' instead of the real things which make up the idea. This produces 'definitions posited by a third party, not self-definitions'. But value, Marx's key economic concept, is itself an idea, an idea which corresponds only roughly to the actual prices of real things. To turn this abstraction, value, into the key concept is a lapse into idealism, if not metaphysics.
28. Marx perhaps realised this. His advice was to start at Chapter 26. Marx to Mrs Wollman, 19/3/77, *CW*, 45, 212. Jenny advised likewise: *CW*, 20, 439–40.
29. Jocasta Shakespeare, 'Nike Work at 16p an hour? Just do it', the *Observer*, 3 December 1995.
30. See, John Roemer, *Free to Lose: An Introduction to Marxist Economic Philosophy*, Radius (Century Hutchinson), London, 1988.
31. *Grundrisse*, *CW*, 28, 195.
32. *Grundrisse*, *CW*, 28, 37–8.
33. Marx, 'Notes on Wagner's *Lehrbuch der politischen Oekonomie*', *CW*, 24, 544–5.
34. Marx is quoting from his earlier work, *Contribution to the Critique of Political Economy*.
35. *Capital*, I, 125.
36. Ibid., 163.
37. Ibid., 177.
38. Ibid., 164–5.
39. 'Economic Manuscript of 1861–3', *CW*, 34, 398.
40. *Capital*, I, 772.

41. *Capital*, III, 341. This chapter (14) lists these factors as: 1. more intense exploitation of labour; 2. reduction of wages below their value; 3. cheapening of the elements of constant capital; 4. the relative surplus population; 5. foreign trade; 6. the increase in share capital. Marx also mentions improved communications and 'revolution in the means of commerce', *Capital*, III, 164.
42. Thomas Sowell, *Marxism: Philosophy and Economics*, George Allen and Unwin, London, 1985, Chapter 6.
43. *Wage Labour and Capital*, *CW*, 9, 218–20.

Engels

1. Preface to *A Contribution to the Critique of Political Economy*, *CW*, 29, 264.
2. Engels to Marx, *CW*, 38, 115.
3. Engels to Marx, 17/11/56, *CW*, 40, 82.
4. *CW*, 42, 63.
5. *CW*, 41, 441–8.
6. *CW*, 43, 170.
7. Engels to Kugelmann, 28/4/71, *CW*, 44, 143.
8. Engels to his mother, 21/10/71, *CW*, 44, 228–9.
9. *CW*, 43, 247, 410, 518.
10. *CW*, 9, 524.
11. *CW*, 43, 541.
12. *Ludwig Feuerbach and the End of Classical German Philosophy*, *CW*, 26, 382.
13. See, for example, *CW*, 47, 17.
14. *Ludwig Feuerbach and the End of Classical German Philosophy*, *CW*, 26, 383.
15. Ibid., 356. See also Ibid., 387.
16. Ibid., 357. To see Engels in the process of developing the idea, see his letter to Marx of 14/7/58, *CW*, 40, 326–7.
17. The quotes are from *Dialectics of Nature*, *CW*, 25, 361.

Marx and Gender

1. Engels, *The Origin of the Family, Private Property and the State*, Lawrence and Wishart, London, 1972, p. 137. Also in *CW*, 26, 181.
2. Ibid., p. 120. Or *CW*, 26, 165.
3. Marx to Engels, *CW*, 39, 509. Also, on grandsons, *CW*, 45, 371; and *CW*, 46, 89.
4. *CW*, 38, 531; and *CW*, 41, 571.
5. Jenny Marx to Liebknecht, 26/5/72, *CW*, 44, 580.
6. Marx to Kugelmann, 12/12/68, *CW*, 43, 184–5.
7. *On the Jewish Question*, *CW*, 3, 172.
8. *EPM*, *CW*, 3, 294.
9. Ibid., 295–6.
10. Fourier, quoted in *The Holy Family*, *CW*, 4, 196.

11. Ibid., 195.
12. Marx, notes about 'Peuchet: On Suicide', *CW*, 4, 605. Cf. his footnote that slaves express their frustration by damaging tools or abusing the cattle in their care. *Capital*, I, 303–4.
13. *The German Ideology*, *CW*, 5, 33.
14. Ibid., 46.
15. Ibid., 180–1.
16. 'Theses on Feuerbach', No. 4, *CW*, 5, 7.
17. *Manifesto of the Communist Party*, *CW*, 6, 501.
18. Marx and Engels, 'Review of Daumer', *CW*, 10, 245.
19. *Capital*, I, 471.
20. Ibid., 516–17. See also Ibid., 364, 599–604 and *Capital*, III, 189–90.
21. Marx, 'Economic Manuscript, 1861–3', *CW*, 33, 491.
22. 'Instructions for the Delegates at the Geneva Conference, 1866', *CW*, 20, 187–8.
23. *Capital*, I, 620.
24. Ibid., 621.
25. *Grundrisse*, *CW*, 29, 278.
26. *The German Ideology*, *CW*, 5, 31.
27. Ibid., 41–2.
28. Ibid., 42–3.
29. 'Theses on Feuerbach', No. 6, *CW*, 5, 4.
30. Shulamith Firestone, *The Dialectic of Sex*, Jonathan Cape, London, 1971, pp. 13–14.
31. *Capital*, I, 718.
32. Selma James points out that his original German word (*einfache*) does not mean simple in the sense of 'uncomplicated', but means more 'the basic unit' of reproduction.
33. Selma James, Introduction to *Power of Women*, quoted in Selma James, *Marx and Feminism*, Crossroads Books, London, n.d., p. 11.
34. See Heidi Hartmann, 'The Unhappy Marriage of Marxism and Feminism', in Lydia Sargent (ed.), *Women and Revolution: A Discussion of the Unhappy Marriage of Marxism and Feminism*, South End Press, Boston MA, 1981.
35. Jenny Marx to Peter Imandt, June 1871, *CW*, 43, 561. Jenny Marx to Liebknecht, 26/5/72, *CW*, 44, 580.
36. 'Civil War In France', *CW*, 22, 311–55.
37. Marx and Engels, 'Review of Daumer', *CW*, 10, 244.
38. *CW*, 38, 119, 408; and *CW*, 43, 113.

Colonialism

1. Marx to Meyer and Vogt, 9/4/70, *CW*, 43, 474–5. See also Ibid., 398.
2. Marx to Engels, 30/7/62, *CW*, 41, 389, 390.
3. Marx to Engels, 11/1/60, *CW*, 41, 4.
4. *Manifesto of the Communist Party*, *CW*, 6, 488.
5. *Wage Labour and Capital*, *CW*, 9, 222–4.
6. *The Poverty of Philosophy*, *CW*, 6, 187.
7. Marx to Lassalle, 22/2/58, *CW*, 40, 270. See also Marx to Engels, 2/4/58, *CW*, 40, 298.

8. 'First International Review', 31/1/50, *CW*, 10, 267.
9. 'Revolution in China and in Europe', June 1853, *CW*, 12, 98.
10. 'The Future Results of the British Rule in India', July 1853, *CW*, 12, 222.
11. Marx, letter to Meyer and Vogt, 9/4/70, *CW*, 43, 473.
12. Marx to Engels, 10/12/69, *CW*, 43, 398.
13. 'Inaugural Address to the First International', 1864, *CW*, 20, 13. See also Marx's address to Abraham Lincoln, that 'single-minded son of the working class', in *CW*, 20, 19–21. And Marx to Lassalle, 28/4/62, *CW*, 41, 357.
14. *The Poverty of Philosophy*, *CW*, 6, 167. See also letter to Annenkov, 28/12/46, *CW*, 38, 101.
15. *Capital*, I, 925.
16. Marx to Kugelmann, 13/12/70, *CW*, 44, 92. Also in his draft to the *Civil War in France*, *CW*, 22, 498, where he uses the word to mean personal dictatorship, capitalist rule and hierarchy.
17. 'Speech on the Question of Free Trade', February 1848, *CW*, 6, 464–5.
18. Marx, 'The Elections in England – Tories and Whigs', 2/8/52, *CW*, 11, 330.
19. Engels to Kautsky, 12/9/82, *CW*, 46, 322. Translation amended.
20. Lenin, *Imperialism: the Highest Stage of Capitalism*, (1917), *Lenin, Collected Works*, Vol. 22, p. 281, Progress Publishers, Moscow, and Lawrence and Wishart, London, 1964.
21. This is the argument of Nathan Rosenberg and L. E. Birdzell in *How the West Grew Rich*, Tauris, London, 1986.
22. Harry Magdoff, *The Age of Imperialism*, Monthly Review Press, New York, 1969.
23. Lenin, *Imperialism: the Highest Stage...*, Preface to French and German editions, July 1920, *Lenin, Collected Works*, Vol. 22, pp. 193–4.
24. Lenin, 'Karl Marx', in *Lenin, Collected Works*, Vol. 21, p. 76.
25. Kwame Nkrumah, *Neo-colonialism: the Last Stage of Imperialism*, Nelson, London, 1965.
26. Figures from Christian Aid and Third World First, 1994.

Religion

1. 'Leading Article in No. 179 of the *Kölnische Zeitung*', *CW*, 1, 200.
2. Ibid., 191.
3. 'Illustrations of the Latest Exercise in Cabinet Style of Frederick William IV', *CW*, 3, 209.
4. 'On the Jewish Question', *CW*, 3, 147–8.
5. 'Contribution to the Critique of Hegel's *Philosophy of Right* [Recht]: Introduction', *CW*, 3, 175.
6. 'Towards a Critique of Hegel's *Philosophy of Right* [Recht]: introduction', in David McLellan, *Karl Marx: Selected Writings*, Oxford University Press, Oxford, 1977. In *CW*, 3, 175–6. The poet Heine had called religion 'mental opium'.
7. 'The Communism of the *Rheinischer Beobachter*', *CW*, 6, 231.

8. Marx to Engels, 17/11/62 and 15/7/74, *CW*, 41, 430; and *CW*, 45, 22. Marx portrays Christianity as inaction and sacrifice of the poor in 'Political Indifferentism', *CW*, 23, 393.
9. *Manifesto of the Communist Party*, *CW*, 6, 508.
10. 'Parliamentary Debates – The Clergy against Socialism', *CW*, 11, 526.
11. Ibid.
12. *Capital*, I, 92, Preface to the first edition.
13. *Capital*, I, 351–2.
14. Ibid., 165.
15. Ludwig Feuerbach, *The Essence of Christianity* (trans. G. Eliot), Harper and Row, New York, 1957, p. 226.
16. 'Critique of the Gotha Programme', *CW*, 24, 98.
17. 'Interview with the *Chicago Tribune*', *CW*, 24, 576.
18. 'Contribution to the Critique of Hegel's *Philosophy of Right* [Recht]', *CW*, 3, 91.
19. Marx, 'The Rhein- und Mosel-Zeitung as Grand Inquisitor', *CW*, 1, 372.
20. *The German Ideology*, *CW*, 5, 56.
21. Marx to Blos, 10/11/77, *CW*, 45, 288.
22. 'Theses on Feuerbach', No. 1, *CW*, 5, 3. See also the work of Alistair Kee.

How (not) to Change the World

1. Marx, 'Theses on Feuerbach', No. 11, *CW*, 5, 5.
2. *Capital*, III, 164.
3. *Manifesto of the Communist Party*, Part 1, *CW*, 6, 483–96.
4. Marx and Engels did have extensive knowledge of America. See their *Letters to Americans, 1848–1895*, International Publishers, New York, 1953.
5. *Communist Manifesto*, *CW*, 6, 488. The original German word 'idotismus' also translates as something like 'privatised isolation', conveying an idea of autonomy and stasis. The word 'idiocy' (Engels' translation) may be unfortunate, but the wider point remains. Marx had little time for peasants. See *CW*, 10, 244–5. It was for Lenin and Mao to reconcile the urban culture of Marxism with the interests of country-people.
6. *The Civil War in France*, *CW*, 22, 331–2.
7. 'On the Jewish Question', *CW*, 3, 147.
8. Shakti Gawain, *Creative Visualisation*, Whatever Publishing Inc., San Rafael CA, 1978, p. 64.

Appendix 1 The Attraction of Marxism

1. *Grundrisse*, *CW*, 28, 99.
2. *The German Ideology*, *CW*, 5, 439.
3. Ibid., 393.
4. *Manifesto of the Communist Party*, *CW*, 6, 506.

5. 'The dialectic is a sort of social X-ray apparatus, enabling us to see the very bones of human society; and to see how they move.' John Strachey, *The Coming Struggle for Power*, Gollancz, London, 1932.

Appendix 2 Violence, Negativity and Failure

1. 'Contribution to the Critique of Hegel's *Philosophy of Right* [Recht]: Introduction', *CW*, 3, 177.
2. Marx, letter to Sorge, 19/10/77, *CW*, 45, 284.
3. See chapter on 'Philosophy'.
4. See Norman Levine, *The Tragic Deception: Marx Contra Engels*, Clio Press, Oxford, 1975.
5. *Manifesto of the Communist Party*, *CW*, 6, 504.
6. *The German Ideology*, *CW*, 5, 49.
7. Richard H. Ullman, *Anglo-Soviet Relations, 1917–1921*, 3 vols, Princeton University Press, New Jersey and Oxford University Press, London, 1961, 1968 and 1973. Michael Kettle, *Russia and the Allies, 1917–1920*, 3 vols, Routledge, London, 1992.
8. *The Civil War in France*, *CW*, 22, 331–3.

Further Reading

Arranged by chapter heading, this gives references to passages in Marx's own work, often short excerpts which are easily readable. After this comes the secondary literature. I suggest reading Marx first, because he is usually more interesting than those who write about him.

A Private Life

The best primary material is the letters of Marx. See especially *Collected Works*, Volumes 38 to 46 and the appendices of Volumes 1 and 3.

'On student days ...' letter home, November 1837, *CW*, 1, 10–21.

Marx and Engels through the Eyes of their Contemporaries, Progress Publishers, Moscow, 1972 (1978 edn).

Briggs, Asa, *Marx in London: An Illustrated Guide*, BBC, London, 1982.

Kapp, Yvonne, *Eleanor Marx*, Lawrence and Wishart, London, 1972.

Liebknecht, Wilhelm, *Karl Marx: Biographical Memoirs*, Kerr, Chicago, 1901.

Nicolaievsky, Boris and Otto Maenchen-Helfen, *Karl Marx: Man and Fighter*, Penguin, Harmondsworth, 1976.

Payne, Robert, ed., *The Unknown Karl Marx*, University of London Press, London, 1972.

Peters, H.F. *Red Jenny: A Life with Karl Marx*, Allen and Unwin, London, 1986.

Schwarzschild, Leopold, *The Red Prussian: The Life and Legend of Karl Marx*, Hamish Hamilton, London, 1948. [This is probably the best 'hatchet job' on Marx.]

Tsuzuki, Chuschichi, *The Life of Eleanor Marx, 1855–1898: A Socialist Tragedy*, Clarendon Press, Oxford, 1967.

A 'World-historical' Life

On the development of his ideas. Preface to the *Contribution to the Critique of Political Economy*, *CW*, 29, 261–5. See also his letter to Nikolai Danielson, 7/10/68, *CW*, 43, 123–4.

At the end of his life. 'Sir Mountstuart Elphinstone Grant Duff's [sic] account of a talk with Karl Marx', 1879, *CW*, 24, 580–2.

Engels' speech at Karl Marx's Funeral, 1883, *CW*, 24, 467–9.
Berlin, Isaiah, *Karl Marx: His Life and Environment*, Oxford
    University Press, London, 1963.
McLellan, David, *Karl Marx: His Life and Thought*, Macmillan,
    London, 1973.
Raddatz, Fritz J., *Karl Marx: A Political Biography*, Weidenfeld and
    Nicolson, London, 1979.
Rubel, Maximilien, *Marx Without Myth: A Chronological Study of
    his Life and Work*, Blackwell, Oxford, 1975.

Unhappiness and Alienation

'Money is the jealous god of Israel' ... 'On the Jewish Question',
    CW, 3, 172.
Marx's main writing on alienation is the section called 'Estranged
    Labour' in the *Economic and Philosophic Manuscripts of 1844*,
    CW, 3, 270–82.
His ideas about private property, alienation and money have an
    intrinsically moral dimension: he is talking about what damages
    the quality of human relations. *EPM*, *CW*, 3, 306–7.
He links the concept of alienation to conflicts of interest, the role
    of the state and the division of labour ... *The German Ideology*,
    CW, 5, 47–8.
In his later work, Marx continues to use the concept explicitly.
    Grundrisse, *CW*, 28, 131–2; and *CW*, 29, 209–10. Also 'Results
    of the Immediate Process of Production', *Capital*, I, 1003–4, or
    CW, 34, 410–11. See also *Capital*, I, 547–9.
The idea is also implicit in his writings on poverty and industrial
    degradation (*Wage Labour and Capital*, *CW*, 9, 203) and child
    labour ('Division of Labour and Mechanical Workshop',
    'Economic Manuscript of 1861–3', *CW*, 33, 492).
Walton, Paul and Andrew Gamble, *From Alienation to Surplus
    Value*, Sheed and Ward, London, 1972.
Foreman, Ann, *Femininity as Alienation: Women and the Family in
    Marxism and Psychoanalysis*, Pluto Press, London, 1977.

How Marx (re)wrote History

Marx's history of the lives of ordinary people has a strong emotional
    and moral dimension. See, for example, his writing about the
    poor in Tudor England. *Capital*, I, 896–7.
On the history of technology and the links between science and
    society. Marx to Engels, 28/1/63, *CW*, 41, 450–1. Cf. Marx,
    'Economic Manuscript of 1861–3', *CW*, 33, 387–425.

Marx wanted to explain how feudalism turns into capitalism. He addresses this in the *Economic and Philosophic Manuscripts, The Poverty of Philosophy*, the *Communist Manifesto* and *Capital*. See *The German Ideology, CW*, 5, 63–74.

On the 'Glorious Revolution' of 1688 and the subsequent rise of manufacture, the world market and the bourgeoisie. 'Review of Guizot', *CW*, 10, 254–5.

History According to Marx

'Circumstances make men just as much as men make circumstances.' *The German Ideology, CW*, 5, 51–5.

Marx explains his approach in a letter to Annenkov, 28/12/46, *CW*, 38, 96–7.

On the social relations between producers. Ancient society, feudal society, bourgeois society are totalities of production relations, each denoting a stage in historical progress. *Wage Labour and Capital, CW*, 9, 211–12.

Cohen, G.A., *Karl Marx's Theory of History: A Defence*, Clarendon Press, Oxford, 1978.

Gottlieb, Roger S., *Marxism, 1844–1990: Origins, Betrayal, Rebirth*, Routledge, London and New York, 1992. (See especially pp. 181–92.)

Jakubowski, Franz, *Ideology and Superstructure in Historical Materialism*, Allison and Busby, London, 1976.

Sayer, Derek, *The Violence of Abstraction: The Analytic Foundations of Historical Materialism*, Basil Blackwell, Oxford, 1987.

Marx's method inspired such classics as:

Hill, Christopher, *The World Turned Upside Down*, Penguin, Harmondsworth, 1978.

Rodney, Walter, *How Europe Underdeveloped Africa*, Bogle-L'Ouverture, London, 1972.

Ste Croix, G.E.M., de, *The Class Struggle in the Ancient Greek World*, Duckworth, London, 1981.

Thompson, E.P., *The Making of the English Working Class*, Gollancz, London, 1963.

Also look at the works of Rodney Hilton and Eric Hobsbawm.

Class and Society

Key works by Marx include:

Manifesto of the Communist Party, CW, 6, 479–519.

The Civil War in France, CW, 22, 307–59.

The Class Struggles in France, CW, 10, 45–145.

The Eighteenth Brumaire of Louis Bonaparte, CW, 11, 103–97.

'Forms preceding capitalist production', a section of the *Grundrisse*, *CW*, 28, 399–439.

Bottomore, Tom and Maximilien Rubel, eds, *Selected Writings in Sociology and Social Philosophy [of Marx]*, Penguin, Harmondsworth, 1963.

On the formation of class society and its possible abolition. *The German Ideology*, *CW*, 5, 77.

The development of unions is crucial for the emancipation of the working class. *The Poverty of Philosophy*, *CW*, 6, 210–11.

'The history of all hitherto existing society is the history of class struggles.' *Manifesto of the Communist Party*, *CW*, 6, 483–5.

The interests of the workers and the bourgeoisie are diametrically opposed. *Wage Labour and Capital*, *CW*, 9, 219–21.

On the peasants. *The Eighteenth Brumaire of Louis Bonaparte*, *CW*, 11, 187–8. Engels shows more faith in the peasants in *The Peasant War in Germany*, 1850, *CW*, 10, 397–489.

Capitalism is special because it is based on 'the free, unobstructed, progressive and universal development of the productive forces'. *Grundrisse*, *CW*, 28, 463–4.

'What makes a class?' *Capital*, III, 1025–6 (that is, the end).

Carling, Alan, *Social Division*, Verso, London, 1991.

Krader, Lawrence, *The Asiatic Mode of Production*, van Gorcum and Comp., Assen, Netherlands, 1975.

Also scan the work of Nicos Poulantzas and Erik Olin Wright.

The Politics of Revolution

The best selections of Marx's political writings are:

Fernbach, D., ed., *Political Writings [of] Karl Marx*, Penguin Books, Harmondsworth, 1992–9.

Vol. 1 *The Revolutions of 1848*

Vol. 2 *Surveys from Exile*

Vol. 3 *The First International and After*

Marx and Engels, *The Socialist Revolution*, Progress Publishers, Moscow, 1978.

For Marx, revolution depends mainly on 'material elements': (a) the 'productive forces' and (b) the 'formation of a revolutionary mass'. *The German Ideology*, *CW*, 5, 51–5.

High praise for the bourgeoisie and for its revolutionary record. *Manifesto of the Communist Party*, *CW*, 6, 486–9.

The bourgeois revolution is inevitably stoking a proletarian one. 'What the bourgeoisie, therefore, produces, above all, is its own grave-diggers.' *Manifesto of the Communist Party*, *CW*, 6, 489–96.

The Paris Commune (1871) was crushed, but Marx was unbowed. *The Civil War in France*, *CW*, 22, 354–5.

What the International achieved. 'Interview with the *Chicago Tribune*', *CW*, 24, 575.
Kimmel, Michael S., *Revolution: A Sociological Interpretation*, Polity Press, Cambridge, 1990.

Socialism and Communism

Marx, Engels, Lenin, *On Scientific Communism*, Progress Publishers, Moscow, 1967. (Mostly Lenin.)
Against bureaucracy. 'Critique of Hegel's *Philosophy of Right*' (Recht)', in McLellan, David, *Karl Marx: Selected Writings*, Oxford University Press, 1977, p. 31. Also *CW*, 3, 46–7.
'The proletariat can thus only exist *world-historically*, just as communism, its activity, can only have a "world-historical" existence.' *The German Ideology*, *CW*, 5, 48–9.
Communism as 'the *world-historical* co-operation of individuals'. *The German Ideology*, *CW*, 5, 51–3.
Communism as the abolition of classes and an end to political power as such. *The Poverty of Philosophy*, *CW*, 6, 211–12.
The 'dictatorship of the proletariat' is 'the necessary transit point to the abolition of class distinctions generally'. *Class Struggles in France, 1848–1850*, *CW*, 10, 127.
On the Paris Commune (1871) as a prototype of socialism. *The Civil War in France*, *CW*, 22, 331–3.
On workers' power. 'Notes on Bakunin's *Statehood and Anarchy*', *CW*, 24, 518–20.

Ideology

On the conflicting world-views of the old landlord class and the new capitalist class. *EPM*, *CW*, 3, 286–8.
'The ideas of the ruling class are in every epoch the ruling ideas ... .' *The German Ideology*, *CW*, 5, 59–60.
'Why the ideologists turn everything upside-down.' *The German Ideology*, *CW*, 5, 92.
On the relationship between language, thought and 'actual life'. *The German Ideology*, *CW*, 5, 446–7.
When writing history, Marx pays a good deal of attention to the 'superstructure' of ideology. *The Eighteenth Brumaire*, *CW* 11, 128.
He has the germ of an idea later developed by Weber, namely that the Puritan emphasis on thrift promotes the rise of capitalism. *Grundrisse*, *CW*, 28, 164. Cf. *EPM*, *CW*, 3, 309.
Collins, Patricia Hill, *Black Feminist Thought*, Routledge, London, 1991.
Eagleton, T., *Ideology: An Introduction*, Verso, London, 1991.

Eccleshall, Robert et al., *Political Ideologies: An Introduction*, Routledge, London, 1994 (2nd edn).

Mannheim, Karl. *Ideology and Utopia: An Introduction to the Sociology of Knowledge*, Routledge and Kegan Paul, London, 1952 (First pub. 1936).

Thompson, John B., *Studies in the Theory of Ideology*, Polity Press, Cambridge, 1984.

Philosophy

Look at Marx's 11 'Theses on Feuerbach', *CW*, 5, 3–5.

Marx summarises his relationship to Hegel and his belief in the revolutionary potential of Hegel's thinking. Postface to the second edition of *Capital*, I, 102–3, 1873.

Marx uses philosophy to discuss and illuminate other subjects. Note how Hegel comes into his account of when precisely a medieval craft-master turns into a modern capitalist. *Capital*, I, 423.

Carver, Terrell, ed., *Texts on Method (of) Karl Marx*, Blackwell, Oxford, 1975.

Korsch, Karl, *Marxism and Philosophy*, New Left Books, London, 1970.

Plamenatz, John, *Karl Marx's Philosophy of Man*, Clarendon Press, Oxford, 1975. (A good overview of the wider issues.)

Smith, Tony, *Dialectical Social Theory and its Critics: From Hegel to Analytical Marxism and Postmodernism*, State University of New York Press, New York, 1993.

Sowell, Thomas, *Marxism: Philosophy and Economics*, Unwin Paperbacks, London, 1986.

Two short introductions to Hegel are: Peter Singer, *Hegel*, Oxford University Press (Past Master Series), 1983; and Lloyd Spencer and Andrzej Krauze, *Hegel for Beginners*, Icon Books, Cambridge, 1996.

Exploitation and Economics

Marx's basic texts on his political economy are *Wage Labour and Capital* (1849) and *Value, Price and Profit* (1865).

The main works are the *Grundrisse* (1857), *Contribution to the Critique of Political Economy* (1859) and, above all, *Capital*. Start with Vol. I (1867). Marx recommended beginning at Chapter 26.

To understand the wider philosophical issues behind Marx's critique of political economy, read the *Economic and Philosophic Manuscripts of 1844*, *CW*, 3.

Early on, Marx notes the problem of monopolies. *EPM*, *CW*, 3, 252.

Some socioeconomic predictions. *Wage Labour and Capital, CW,* 9, 227.

On the size and scope of his project. Marx to Lassalle, 22/2/58, *CW,* 40, 270. See also Marx to Engels, 2/4/58, *CW,* 40, 298. *Grundrisse, CW,* 28, 195.

The concept of value. 'Value, Price and Profit', *CW,* 20, 118–24.

On the inter-relations between production, distribution, exchange and consumption. *Grundrisse, CW,* 28, 36–7.

On improved 'means of communication', how they boost profit margins, off-setting the tendency of the rate of profit to fall. *Capital,* III, 164.

On 'commodity fetishism'. *Capital,* I, 164–5.

There are many useful summaries and guides:

Blaug, Mark, *A Methodological Appraisal of Marxian Economics,* North Holland Publishing Company, Amsterdam, 1980.

Brus, Wlodzimierz and Kazimierz Laski, *From Marx to the Market: Socialism in Search of an Economic System,* Clarendon Press, Oxford, 1989.

Burkitt, Brian, *Radical Political Economy: An Introduction to the Alternative Economics,* Wheatsheaf, Harvester, Brighton, 1984.

Dobb, Maurice, *Marx as an Economist,* Lawrence and Wishart, London, 1977 (First pub. 1943).

Fine, Ben, *Marx's Capital,* 3rd edn, Macmillan, London, 1989.

Jalée, Pierre, *How Capitalism Works,* Monthly Review Press, New York, 1977.

Junankar, P.N., *Marx's Economics,* Philip Allan, Oxford, 1982.

Linder, Marc, *Anti-Samuelson* (2 vols), Pluto Press, London and Urizen, New York. (This is a critique of Paul Samuelson and conventional micro and macro economics.)

Mandel, Ernest, *Late Capitalism,* Verso, London, 1978.

Roemer, John, *Free to Lose: An Introduction to Marxist Economic Philosophy,* Radius, Century Hutchinson, London, 1988.

Rosdolsky, Roman, *The Making of Marx's Capital,* Pluto Press, London, 1977. (First pub. 1968).

Sherman, Howard J., *Foundations of Radical Political Economy,* M.E. Sharpe, New York, 1987.

Engels

Have a look at Engels' main works and consider how they differ from Marx's.

Engels on Manchester. A choice passage ... *The Condition of the Working Class in England,* Penguin Classics, London, 1987, p. 89 (First pub. 1845).

On the moral character of English and Irish, bourgeoisie and proletariat. Ibid., 150–4.

On the 'negation of the negation'. *Anti-Dühring*, *CW*, 25, 125–32.

On the future ... 'we shall find ourselves compelled to make communist experiments and leaps which no one knows better than ourselves to be untimely'. Engels to Weydemeyer, 12/4/53, *CW*, 39, 308–9.

The two best short introductions are:

Carver, Terrell, *Engels*, Past Masters Series, Oxford University Press, Oxford, 1981.

McLellan, David, *Engels*, Modern Masters Series, Fontana, London, 1977.

Longer works are:

Carver, Terrell, *Friedrich Engels: His Life and Thought*, Macmillan, London, 1989.

Carver, Terrell, *Marx and Engels: The Intellectual Relationship*, Wheatsheaf, Brighton, 1983.

Levine, Norman, *The Tragic Deception: Marx contra Engels*, Clio Books, Oxford, 1975.

Rigby, S.H., *Engels and the Formation of Marxism: History, Dialectics and Revolution*, Manchester University Press, Manchester, 1992.

Marx and Gender

Women and Communism: Selections from the Writings of Marx, Engels, Lenin and Stalin, Greenwood Press, Westport (Conn.), 1973. (Reprint of 1950 edn published by Lawrence and Wishart, London.) Apart from the intrinsic interest of the selections, the book shows, contrary to its intention, how Marxists tried to appropriate 'women's issues'.

For Engels the obvious book is: *The Origin of the Family, Private Property and the State*, Lawrence and Wishart, London, 1972 (First pub. 1884). Another way to see Engels' views and the extent to which he both studies and overlooks women's lives is *The Condition of the Working Class in England*, First pub. 1845. Penguin, London 1987.

'The direct, natural and necessary relation of person to person is the *relation of man to woman*.' *Economic and Philosophic Manuscripts of 1844*, *CW*, 3, 295–6.

On abolishing the family. *Manifesto of the Communist Party*, *CW*, 6, 501–2.

On conditions faced by working class women. *Capital*, I, 364. See also *Capital*, III, 189–90.

Engels thought that in the old communistic household women's work was fully valued. Only with the arrival of the patriarchal, monogamous family, did a woman's work becomes a private service for her husband. *The Origin of the Family, Private Property and the State*, Lawrence and Wishart, London, 1972, p. 137 (First pub. 1884). Or *CW*, 26, 181.

Read almost any works by Alexandra Kollontai, for example, *Communism and the Family*, Socialist Workers Party, London, 1984.

Sargent, Lydia, ed., *The Unhappy Marriage of Marxism and Feminism*, Pluto Press, London, 1981. The lead essay of the same title by Heidi Hartmann is followed by a debate on class and patriarchy. The book is published in the USA as *Women and Revolution*, South End Press, Boston.

Guettel, Charnie, *Marxism and Feminism*, Canadian Women's Educational Press, Toronto, 1974.

Vogel, Lise, *Marxism and the Oppression of Women*, Pluto Press, London, 1983.

A creative and very readable application of Marx's theory is: James, Selma, *Marx and Feminism*, Crossroads Books, Kings Cross Women's Centre, PO Box 287, London, NW6 5QU (ISBN 09517775 5 6).

A good introduction to gender as such is: Richardson, Diane and Victoria Robinson, eds, *Introducing Women's Studies*, London, Macmillan, 1993.

Firestone, Shulamith, *The Dialectic of Sex*, Jonathan Cape, London, 1971.

Phillips, Eileen, ed., *The Left and the Erotic*, Lawrence and Wishart, London, 1983.

Reich, Wilhelm, *Sex-pol: Essays 1929–1934*, Vintage Books, New York, 1972.

Rose, Hilary, *Love, Power and Knowledge*, Polity Press, Cambridge, 1994.

Colonialism

Marx and Engels, *On Colonialism*, Lawrence and Wishart, London, 1959.

Marx and Engels, *Ireland and the Irish Question*, London, Lawrence and Wishart, 1971.

On the world market and the globalisation of capitalism. 'Speech on the Question of Free Trade', February 1848, *CW*, 6, 463–5.

On the innately expansionist tendencies of capitalism. *Manifesto of the Communist Party*, *CW*, 6, 487–8.

On the different interest groups involved in colonialism and the long-term results of colonial rule. 'The Future Results of the British Rule in India', July 1853, *CW*, 12, 218–21.

On slavery. *Capital*, II, 555.

Trying to calculate how much wealth England was extracting from its colonies. *Capital*, III, 725.

On the exploitation of the colonies, the accumulation of capital and the growth of the capitalist system. With reference to Dutch colonialism in Java; corruption in the English East India Company; plantation colonies in the West Indies; genocide in New England; and English participation in the slave trade. *Capital*, I, Chapter 31, 'The Genesis of the Industrial Capitalist', pp. 916–26.

'The English WORKING CLASS will *never accomplish anything* BEFORE IT HAS GOT RID OF IRELAND.' Marx to Engels, 10/12/69, *CW*, 43, 398. See also Marx to Meyer and Vogt, 9/4/70, *CW*, 43, 473–5. And *CW*, 46, 40.

Clark, John, *For Richer, For Poorer: Western Connections with World Hunger*, Oxfam, Oxford, 1986.

Coote, Belinda, *The Trade Trap: Poverty and the Global Commodity Markets*, Oxfam, Oxford 1992.

George, Susan, *A Fate Worse than Debt*, Penguin, London, 1988.

Lenin, *Imperialism: The Highest Stage of Capitalism*, Progress Publishers, Moscow, 1982.

Nkrumah, Kwame, *Neo-colonialism: The Last Stage of Imperialism*, Nelson, London, 1965.

Mosse, Julia Cleves, *Half the World, Half a Chance: An Introduction to Gender and Development*, Oxfam, Oxford, 1992.

Ross, Robert and Kent Trachte, *Global Capitalism: The New Leviathan*, SUNY Press, Albany, USA, 1990.

Said, Edward W., *Culture and Imperialism*, Vintage, London, 1993.

Said, Edward W., *Orientalism: Western Conceptions of the Orient*, Penguin, London, 1995 (First pub. 1978).

Wallerstein, Immanuel, *The Modern World System*, Vols 1, 2 and 3. Academic Press, New York, 1974, 1980, 1989.

Also look at the work on 'underdevelopment' of André Gunder Frank, Samir Amin, Arghiri Emmanuel and Eduardo Galeano.

Religion

Marx and Engels, *On Religion*, Progress, Moscow, 1957.

Marx's school writing indicates a devout faith. *CW*, 1, 639.

'We turn theological questions into secular ones.' 'On the Jewish Question', *CW*, 3, 151.

'Man makes religion, religion does not make man.' 'Contribution to the Critique of Hegel's *Philosophy of Right* (Recht): Introduction', *CW*, 3, 175–6.

Marx criticises Christianity because 'it regarded our flesh, our desires as something foreign to us'; and 'it does not go beyond mere moral injunctions, which remain ineffective in real life'. *The German Ideology*, *CW*, 5, 254.

Marx was quick to seize on the works of contemporaries which showed the evils of the Church. 'Minutes of Marx's Report to the London German Workers' Educational Society', 30/11/47. *CW*, 6, 630–1.

Engels, *On the History of Early Christianity*, *CW*, 27, 447–52.

An article on the 'Anti-Church Movement', *CW*, 14, 302–7.

Bloch, Ernst, *Man on his Own: Essays in the Philosophy of Religion*, Herder and Herder, New York, 1970.

Evans, Donald, *Communist Faith and Christian Faith*, SCM Press, London, 1965.

Gorringe, T.J., *Capital and the Kingdom*, Orbis/SPCK, London, 1994.

Hebblethwaite, Peter. *The Christian–Marxist Dialogue and Beyond*, Darton Longman and Todd, London, 1977.

Kautsky, Karl, *Foundations of Christianity*, International Publishers Company, London, 1925. (Especially the final chapter on 'Christianity and Socialism'.)

Kee, Alistair, *Domination or Liberation: The Place of Religion in Social Conflict*, SCM Press, London, 1986.

Kee, Alistair, *Marx and the Failure of Liberation Theology*, SCM Press, London, 1990.

Kolakowski, Leszek, *Religion*, Fontana, Glasgow, 1982.

Lash, Nicholas, *A Matter of Hope*, Darton Longman Todd, London, 1983.

Ling, Trevor, *Buddha, Marx and God: Some Aspects of Religion in the Modern World*, Macmillan, London, 1979.

Ling, Trevor, *Karl Marx and Religion*, Macmillan, London, 1980.

MacIntyre, Alasdair, *Marxism and Christianity*, Duckworth, London, 1983 (First pub. 1968).

McLellan, David, *Marxism and Religion: A Description and Assessment of the Marxist Critique of Christianity*, Macmillan, Basingstoke, 1987.

Miranda, Jose P., *Communism in the Bible*, SCM Press, London, 1981.

How (not) to Change the World

Blackwell, Trevor and Jeremy Seabrook, *The Revolt Against Change: Towards a Conserving Radicalism*, Vintage, London, 1993.

Cooney, Robert and Helen Michalowskii, *The Power of the People: Active Non-Violence in the United States*, New Society Publishers, Philadelphia, 1987.

Grundmann, Reiner, *Marxism and Ecology*, Clarendon Press, Oxford, 1991.

Hayek, F.A., *The Fatal Conceit: The Errors of Socialism*, Routledge, London, 1988.

Pegg, Mike, *The Positive Planet*, Enhance Ltd., Leamington Spa, 1993. (A practical manual, encouraging people to use their talents in their daily work.)

Randle, Michael, *Civil Resistance*, Fontana, London, 1994.

Schluter, Michael and David Lee, *The R Factor*, Hodder and Stoughton, London, 1993. (Proposes something 'beyond capitalism and Marxism': Relationism.)

The Attraction of Marxism

Almond, Gabriel A., *The Appeals of Communism*, Princeton University Press, Princeton NJ and Oxford University Press, Oxford, 1954.

Aron, Raymond, *The Opium of the Intellectuals*, Secker and Warburg, London, 1957.

Gornick, Vivian, *The Romance of American Communism*, Basic Books, New York, 1977.

Koestler, Arthur, *The God that Failed*, The Right Book Club, London, 1950.

Index

177